'the social agent' 2.0 update

the evolution of digital marketing

Tony Giordano

ISBN: 1982051833

ISBN 13: 9781982051839

This book is dedicated to my amazing mother, Mary Colleen Giordano, a woman who always made me feel like Superman. Regardless of my failures growing up, she never told me to get back up; instead, I would have to come to that conclusion myself. When I asked her why, she put it simply: "You will never be one that I worry about; I already know you are not a quitter and will succeed. Know it yourself, son."

I will miss you forever, Wonder Woman. You made me the father and man I am today. Watching you fight gave me an inner strength that I didn't know I had. *I think of you every day, every sunset and sunrise; I think of you every time I see the blue of the ocean, when I see your stunning eyes.*

Mamma, ti voglio bene con tutto il mio course (*I love you with all my heart, Mom*). Be in peace...

In loving Memory of Mary Colleen Giordano
4.25.58–4.12.13

acknowledgments of gratitude

The author has several people he would like to thank...

Thank you to my two sons, Michael and Christopher, for being such well-behaved young men. You fuel me every day to pave as many roads as I can in front of you so your journey in life isn't too bumpy. I am so proud of both of you, and want to make sure you never forget to never quit, and always follow your heart.

Special thanks to my amazing and stunning lady, London Howe. Besides building me a bunker where no one can distract me, you truly are my "significant" other. You bring me balance and a sense of purpose on a side of my life I have often neglected, and you help me to enjoy the moment. Yet you still support my drive and desire to always be in my bunker writing on my walls. ☺ I love you, Sugar.

Thank you to my "godfather," Uncle Mike! You played such a massive role in writing my first book, and I will keep your legacy alive. Rest in peace.

Thank you once again to John Hildebrand and Clint Eastwood for your wicked photography skills in capturing the front cover iPad image.

Thank you to all of my coaching clients over the last few years. I don't have enough room to name you all here individually, but I want you to know we learn from each other, and you've personally added to my own growth—and I'm grateful for you. Now get back to work. ☺

Thank you to my amazing staff for the priceless leverage that you continue to provide to my dreams and goals. No one succeeds alone, and I am often reminded of that through all you do for me.

Thank you to all my speaking relationships, affiliates, and partners for your continued support and the opportunities you graciously have brought me.

the '*news feed*' of contents

share—timeline

Time line—what a broad word, right? Most people immediately think of Facebook when they hear it now. There is no question I have had quite a time line in my real life. Personally, today, when I hear the word, I initially think of the birth of my digital identity—my "digital twin," if you will.

Tony Giordano just joined Facebook—December 22, 2008

Wasn't that long ago. However, in this introduction of the book, I want to talk about a different time line. I want to talk about the few years prior to that, which eventually led up to the birth of my digital identity.

To not go too far back, and to make a long story short, let's start with 2004. By the age of twenty-six, I had made my first million as a mortgage broker after starting in lending in 1998 as a twenty-one-year-old loan officer. Although I had an extremely successful young career underway, mostly fueled by a post-9/11 economy and a very lenient lending industry, I had no idea what would happen just a few years later. What I did know—or assumed, that is—was that I was unbreakable. Life would be great and dandy forever as far as I was concerned. Yeah, right! This arrogant way of thinking is what led to me developing a different way of thinking and developing a statement I truly believed and wanted to help others always remember. I will share that quote after describing what I experienced.

After closing the best year of my career, I was now entering what would be a very interesting 2007, to say the least. In the first half of the year, all my business was still coming in through word of mouth, strict daily lead generation in the morning, and building "real-life" relationships. Most of my clients that year comprised of celebrities, athletes, and executives. However, by the second half of the year, all my business wasn't coming from anywhere—it was gone entirely. Instead of hearing my brand-new 2007 debut iPhone ringing, I heard crickets mostly. Even though I had some of my largest transactions of my career close that same year, I was chasing overleveraged debt. The inner feeling that I had "real assets," like my real estate holdings, art, jewelry, cars, boats, etc., well, that was diminishing before my eyes. Why? Well, the one thing in that last sentence that is missing is "liquid assets," and I had zero left. I put all my liquid in my remodeled homes or stupid "impulse-buy" toys. At the same time as all of this, I was going through a divorce, and the banking industry was about to crash and cause another great depression. Now the realization of something catastrophic was entering my mind: What am I going to do? How will I not only survive but continue to dominate in my industry?

It obviously was not pretty going into 2008. We were at the beginning of what would be a massive banking and economic crisis. *The Big Short* was underway. Most have us have heard of the Hollywood movie; a lot of us have seen it. If you have not, you should.

Now, mind you, at this time, my main online identity or presence, if you will, was a Myspace profile that my friend helped me set up to meet people. Although it was fun, different, and kind of cool, I looked at it in a very different way than most users at the time. To me, it was a chance to maybe build a relationship I would have never had. Whether for my personal dating life, a new friend, or maybe a new potential client, I saw the opportunity, and it seemed limitless.

Throughout 2008, it only got worse for me, though. My industry became a ghost town, and my income dropped 80 percent yet again! I had to "short-sale" my homes, trade in assets for lesser assets, and ultimately go into what I call today "tactical survival mode." Every decision I was making was a methodical one. I had to think way in the future to what the outcomes would be from the simplest decisions and whether those decisions would help in my overall survival in the industry—and, eventually, an even more powerful line of business.

As the months came and went that year, lending only got worse. I couldn't get anyone approved, it seemed, especially my clientele, who were mostly seeking super jumbo loan amounts. I was, without question, losing my passion for the business. By September of 2008, everything was gone. Houses, boats, cars, and any assets I may have had were all but history now. I was down to my old pickup truck I owned free and clear that I used to take my dog Roxy to the beach in, and what was left of my surfboard collection. In all honesty, though, that is all a SoCal guy needs anyway. Truck, surfboard, dog, CHECK! ☺ Yet, I had no money to my name, and I was bartending at night to put food on the table for my sons. However, giving up just wasn't an option.

I can remember several times paying for a potential client's lunch with the last $33 in my bank account, literally checking my bank account on my phone to make sure I could cover it. You want to talk about getting out of your comfort zone? Trust me, I know it all too well.

Seriously, though, how was I going to rebound? What would it take? I always had a natural ability in marketing and advertising myself, which proved very beneficial in my ten-year mortgage career. I had unique ads that I would run that set me apart from most of my competition. So how would I use these marketing skills to recover from the crash? I had no money, so I couldn't run print marketing and advertisements consistently.

Well, here we are: it is now December 22, 2008, and I decide to join Facebook, as everyone is telling me it is better than Myspace. Well, everyone was right. It was no doubt better than Myspace. I saw it as a massive marketing opportunity. The system within Facebook was truly genius. Within a few months on the network, I had a few hundred "friends," and I took my marketing skills and started implementing them on the network. However, I was all over the place. I would post a clever comment about mortgage lending to try to maybe get a client, but then I would also post not exactly the most professional pictures. Not knowing the potential of what networks like Facebook and LinkedIn could actually do for my business, I continued with that approach through 2009.

By spring of 2009, I could barely pay rent on time, and I probably funded a loan once a month at the most throughout the months leading up to October 2009. By that time, I was two months behind on rent with no clue when the next commission check would come through. I know what you're probably thinking: "Tony, why didn't you just throw in the towel and find a full-time job somewhere?" Well, because deep down, I truly feel that there is only one word that stands between failure and success, and that is quitting. I was not going to quit. I welcome failure as long as I am willing to learn from it and never fear it.

In October of 2009, I finally decided I was going to switch to the real estate sales side of the business and leave the real estate finance side. I already had my real estate license as a mortgage broker, so I went straight into selling homes. The first week as an agent, I started researching the biggest real estate agents (top 1 percent) in LA on Google. As I looked at their online image, I saw one common aspect between almost all of them. They all had fully custom, gorgeous websites. While researching them, I remember seeing an article from the National Association of Realtors about the importance of being online in your business and that the majority of consumers were looking for their property and/or even agents online. So even though I was two months behind on rent, I immediately, after reading it, called a web design company and asked them to take my boring and very inactive website at the time, TonyGiordano.net, and make it look like a million-dollar website. Perception is everything, and I knew if my online presence looked strong, it would eventually attract the leads and business—the same way a nice car would have helped a professional's business twenty years ago. In October 2009, my website finally launched after scraping up the remaining money I had to pay toward it. The switch to real estate agent was official, and I was a lender no more.

If you read my first edition of *the social agent*, then you know that around this same time in October 2009, I went to a class called Facebook 101. There I learned just how powerful this "new era of social networking" online really was. I learned that although a Facebook business page is important, sales professionals should have a minimum of two thousand friends on their personal Facebook friend pages as well.

I implemented that strategy, and within thirty days, I got a multimillion-dollar listing from a complete stranger I had never met in person, but we were friends on Facebook. The rest was history at that point. By the end of my rookie year in 2010, I started speaking nationally on the topic of online media. I was rebuilding. I knew I wasn't going to succumb to the economic crisis—or anything, for that matter. Long, and I mean very long story short, by the end of 2011 I had multimillion-dollar real estate listings all over the world. I finished my book, *the social agent*, which would become a bestseller in under three years. Today, I am asked frequently, "If there was one word you would say is the main reason you were able to rebuild everything, what would it be?" My answer is always the same: "Online." Online presence was everything. The difference for it working with me, though, was that I understood the human side to it and ignored the tech side to it. Now, today, I have one goal year after year, and it never changes: growth. That is my goal every year—five years, ten years—simply growth in all things, both personal and in business.

Human Being

Anthony Vincent Giordano

Born August 11, 19—☺

Beverly Hills, California

7 lbs. 9 oz, Bald w/ Hazel Eyes

Digital Being

Tony Giordano

Born online December 22, 2008

Facebook.com

Profile Picture: **Still** Bald, w/ Hazel Eyes

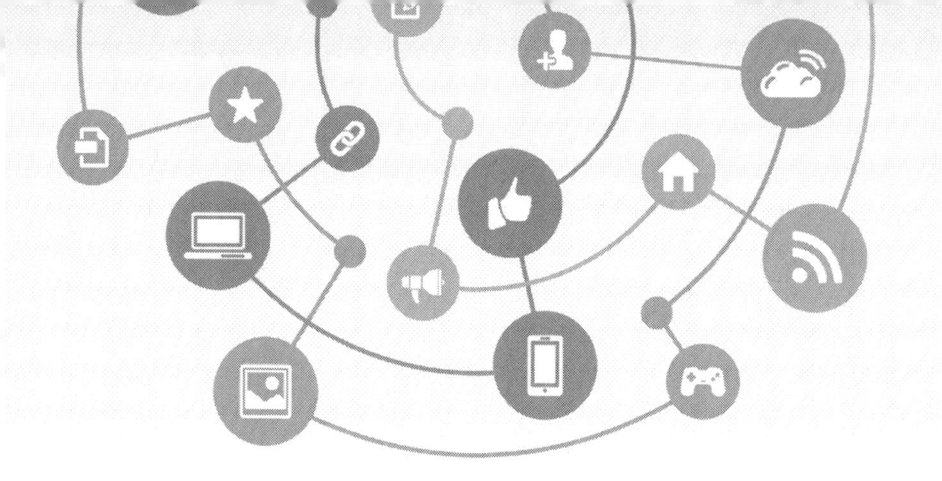

CHAPTER 1

the digital evolution

Scan to *Follow* me everywhere...

Now, regarding my first book, *the social agent: the new era of social networking*, I really don't even like calling it a book as much as it is a guide that is a great first step before reading this book. It is an opening of the mind, if you will, on how simple online networking is and how effective it is when you take a human approach to the digital world and *why*. However, in this second edition, 2.0 update, we are going to be discussing the importance of being active on multiple networks and/or sites and reveal some more *why*, along with a lot of *what*, *where*, *when*, and *how*. This chapter is to show you the evolution over the last few years of big networks and their niches as the FAB 5 evolved into the MAGNIFICENT 7, then the ONLINE | ON-9, and then the PERFECT 10, as I like to call them. It is also to show you that even though it is important to have them all, you will spend more or less time in each one, depending on what purpose it serves you or can serve your brand. Let's start with the FAB 5.

• • •

FAB 5

FACEBOOK: The "Social" Network
TWITTER: The "News" Network
GOOGLE+: The "I Have No Clue" Network
YOUTUBE: The "Video" Network
LINKEDIN: The "Professionals" Network

These are the FAB 5, and you can reference their nicknames that I have given them based on what their real purpose is—like Google+, the "I have no clue" network. ☺ Don't worry, I will explain that in chapter 9. Throughout this book we will reveal the niche of each one and what the true approach is to building relationships and your brand in each of them. They are the FAB 5 because they have the greatest niches over all other networks, and sites like Instagram, WhatsApp, Snapchat, Pinterest, and more have spawned from the Fab 5. MySpace may have had the initial popularity, but Facebook quickly mastered and innovated the social media scene and became global. Facebook is the giant. It is not "a" social network; it is "the" social network. There is nobody that even comes close to touching Facebook's dominance. Do you think I'm wrong? I'll give you over a billion reasons why I'm not: Facebook has over a billion more people than any other social network. Not millions more—a *billion* more. A billion more than Instagram, a billion more than Pinterest, a billion more than Twitter, a billion more than...you name it. There is no reason that Facebook won't eventually have the entire online world population of almost four billion. Facebook is the king. Actually, it is the king and queen. I am sure you've heard others say, and might be thinking to yourself right now, "Well, the teenagers and younger generations are leaving Facebook, Tony; they're going to Instagram and Snapchat. So why should I do Facebook if the next generation doesn't like Facebook?" Of course younger generations left Facebook a few years ago. They didn't want to be friends with Grandma and Grandpa online. So they flooded the gates of Instagram. Then Mom and Dad started following them on Instagram, so they flooded the gates of SnapChat. Here is the critical fact you must realize, though. What do the majority of teenagers need social media for? What it started out as in universities across America is what they need it for.

- ☐ Who's Dating, Who's Not
- ☐ Self-Expression (In Ways They Shouldn't)
- ☐ Wannabe Musicians
- ☐ Wannabe Supermodels
- ☐ Selfies
- ☐ Case of the Mondays Selfie
- ☐ Taco Tuesday Selfie
- ☐ New Hairstyle Wednesday Selfie
- ☐ Kissy-Face Lip-Smacking Thursday Selfie
- ☐ Thank God It's Friday Selfie
- ☐ Saturday Date Night "Check Me Out" Selfie
- ☐ Sunday Funday Selfie
- ☐ Animated Flowers on Her Forehead
- ☐ Cartoon Puppy Dog Tongues Hanging Out of Her Mouth

That's why they need social media. Do the majority of seventeen-year-olds need social media to build relationships within a massive network like Facebook so they can sell their product at a higher level? Do they need it to build a brand or the productivity of a business or corporation? No, they don't. Most don't even have careers yet, and you're going to let a teenager be the reason you stop using something and start using something else? Remember what they need it for. I speak for the business graduate classes of some of the largest universities in America, and I learn from the younger generation as much as they learn from me. However, one of the statements I make onstage many times at these universities, I say with a factual confidence: "Ninety-five percent of this auditorium doesn't know a fraction of what I know about social media, and I'm forty!"

Why can I say that with confidence? Because the majority of that generation only need to use social media for its minimum purposes stated on the previous page. It's the same on the older scale too. Would you let a much older generation who's been in real estate or sales for thirty-plus years, who don't even understand social networks, tell you that they don't work? Be careful who you are learning and taking advice from. Now you may be thinking, "OK, Tony, there's a hundred social networks out there, and I get the FAB 5. But if I wanted to have presence on two more social networks, and I didn't know which ones to pick out of one hundred sites out there, which ones would you add to the FAB 5?" That's where I take you to the MAGNIFICENT 7, and we add Pinterest and Instagram to the group.

MAGNIFICENT 7

FACEBOOK: The "Social" Network
TWITTER: The "News" Network
GOOGLE+: The "I Have No Clue" Network
YOUTUBE: The "Video" Network
LINKEDIN: The "Professionals" Network
INSTAGRAM: The "Visual" Network
PINTEREST: The "Interest" Network

It's not because they're better than the other big social networks per se; it is because they also have great niches, and they've grown into global marketing giants—especially if you know what to do once inside them. These are major online platforms. Instagram alone has risen as the largest visual network in the world. That means it is self-expression visually. Every single national and international brand you see driving down the street or online is selling more product online today simply because of Pinterest traffic to its website, more than ever before. Louis Vuitton, Chanel, Tiffany, Nike, Reebok, VANS, Quiksilver... whatever retail brand you can think of right now is pushing more product online through people who came to its site through Pinterest. If you know how to brand and market yourself as a real estate agent by showing and educating consumers on interior design, furniture, exterior styles, architecture, do it yourself, or more, and you become known as this Pinterest profile that people can go to for this reference, it is an opportunity to build your brand. There is even benefit to go as far as pinning photos of your listings from your website, making you even more relevant.

Want more? Are you thinking to yourself once again, "If I wanted to do two more and start having presence inside them, what are they?" That's where I take you to the ON-9, and we will add WeChat and WhatsApp to the mix.

• • •

ONLINE | ON-9

FACEBOOK: The "Social" Network
TWITTER: The "News" Network
GOOGLE+: The "I Have No Clue" Network
YOUTUBE: The "Video" Network
LINKEDIN: The "Professionals" Network
INSTAGRAM: The "Visual" Network
PINTEREST: The "Interest" Network
WHATSAPP: The "Message" Network
WECHAT: The "Story" Network

WhatsApp and WeChat are social messaging apps for instant messaging, chatting, and so forth, and they are also dominant apps and platforms for the purpose of going mobile and making sure you are accessible in the latest evolution of communication, both now and in the future.

They are social networks of their own, but in very different ways. For now, until you get to that chapter, just think of WeChat like Facebook and Facebook Messenger for China. Think of WhatsApp as an app you download that replaces the text app (green square) that came with your phone. It's like texting on steroids—and a more effective way of communicating globally. An argument could be made, and you may be thinking it now: "Tony, where is Snapchat?" Fine, then, let's say you wanted me to add that to the list, we would then make it to the...

• • •

PERFECT 10

FACEBOOK: The "Social" Network
TWITTER: The "News" Network
GOOGLE+: The "I Have No Clue" Network
YOUTUBE: The "Video" Network
LINKEDIN: The "Professionals" Network
INSTAGRAM: The "Visual" Network
PINTEREST: The "Interest" Network
WECHAT: The "Story" Network
WHATSAPP: The "Message" Network
SNAPCHAT: The "No Need" Network

Snapchat's niche is short, viral videos that hook your interest. It's also mostly still a social platform for a younger generation of users to share their personal daily stories with their closest friends and family. Big business today like CNBC, CNN, and Fox News have Snapchat accounts; however, their traffic on Snapchat is in no way equal to the traffic they have on platforms like Facebook, Twitter, YouTube, and others. Snapchat needs to compete with the other big platforms better than it is at the moment. Or it may be acquired eventually. You can see a big push right now with Facebook owning Instagram and pushing video inside Instagram at a very, very high level. They now have stories within Instagram just like Snapchat. Instagram has already started to gain a lot of steam in advertising and sponsored ads inside the platform. So it's going to be interesting to see what happens to Snapchat and whether it can have a significant purpose in building your brand and productivity. This book's purpose is not to tell you that you must use all these networks to build your brand. This book is about where you should spend the majority of your time for the highest return on investment (ROI). For the time being, you need to have an account with Snapchat and make sure you're familiar with the app for whatever the next evolution of Snapchat will be. I used to have the social media network Periscope in the ONLINE I ON-9 group. Periscope's niche was that it was the first to have live video streaming. It came on the scene a few years ago and exploded very quickly, but only people in the tech and social media world really knew Periscope existed. As it gained popularity, Twitter took notice of Periscope, and as we think of *live* broadcasting when we think of the news, Twitter purchased Periscope. Since that acquisition, Twitter now has live tweeting integrated into its platform. However, who has already stolen the word "live" when you think of "*live*"? Facebook, right? Shows you the power of marketing, doesn't it? You need to make sure you have an account on all these platforms we just went over. Main reason: you need to be searchable and findable in anything that has hundreds of millions of people in it. That is just smart business. Yes, there are dozens and dozens more "social networks" out there; however, these we just went over are the largest ones with the best niches for growing relationships and a brand. For the sake of this book, though, we are going to focus and spend most of our time on the most effective networks for building your brand and business.

Throughout this read, you will see experiences and examples that I have used and taught in my own industry of real estate. I will also include examples of techniques for multiple industries. Anyone who relies on reaching more people in order to grow their business, whether they are a business owner or a salesperson, the approach to building their brand is the same. The more people you build relationships with, the easier you can build your brand. Why?

Sales is a ________ game.

Exactly, go after the numbers. Sales is a contact sport. *Period.* If you do go after the numbers online, you will crush your competition. Whether you sell or provide retail, homes, loans, insurance, medical supplies, cars, interior design, nutrition, fashion, training, dentistry, legal counsel, travel, electronics, and so on and so on, your job is to get in front of people and tell them what you do.

> "*Never* assume where a lead is going to come from. Always just remember, they come from humans."
> — #TonyG

I have hours upon hours of curriculum on every single one of these PERFECT 10 networks. Sometimes, even days of curriculum. On my Facebook friend page alone, I have three full days of curriculum. On my Facebook business page, three full days. LinkedIn, three full days. Twitter, two full days, and days of curriculum for most of theses networks. Within these networks I coach agents on advanced strategies and techniques that continue to increase their ROI time and time again. The digital world is here—the digital neighborhood of social networks. The digital ways we communicate globally, or the modern-day store we shop at, like Amazon, only become a part of our lives more and more. This is the digital world that you must take seriously, and must adapt to, across many facets of your life and business. Are you evolving with the evolution? I know you are a human being, but are you also a digital being? It amazes me what we have achieved and created in the digital world and the power it has to evolve on its own.

THE BIRTH AND EVOLUTION OF CRYPTOCURRENCY

I am currently writing a book on the topic of cryptocurrency. Words like digital currency, cryptocurrency, Blockchain, Bitcoin, Ethereum, and Litecoin you are more than likely continuing to hear about. There are more and more posts, tweets, shares, and news about how many people are making massive returns on their investments into cryptocurrency. I want to at least share with you the gist of what it is so it benefits your business now, giving you some level of knowledge and understanding on it. Maybe you have even researched it and tried to learn about it, or you might even be one of the very few people who know a lot about it already. In any case, let's talk about it briefly, as I feel it goes hand in hand with being a social and digital agent or broker today, as well as a savvy buyer or seller. Everything about this book is designed to help grow your business in the digital world, which now also has its own currency—and at the rate it is going, it will play a part in the future of real estate even more than it has already started to.

WHAT IS CRYPTOCURRENCY (DIGITAL CURRENCY)?

Cryptocurrency (digital currency) has been around for years. A few years ago, a gentlemen and/or group under the alias name Satoshi Nakamoto, who remains unidentified, created cryptocurrency. Despite how many sceptics have criticized and advised caution when it comes to cryptocurrency, there have been many experts who have shown the currency's value. These experts in the field have been validated time and time again with the consistent growth in value, technology, buy-in, and popularity the currency continues to create against all odds.

cryp·to·cur·ren·cy

ˈkriptōˌkərənsē/

noun

a digital currency in which encryption techniques are used to regulate the generation of units of currency and verify the transfer of funds, operating independently of a central bank.

https://en.wikipedia.org/wiki/Cryptocurrency

How 'bout in English? Cryptocurrency is like any currency, really. Gold, silver, dollars, euros, francs, dinars, and all other currencies in the world are given a value that we as people have given those currencies. What is a dollar [USD] even worth, without gold to back it up? We don't even have enough gold to back up the $20 trillion of currency debt in the world. That is why the piece of paper says "FEDERAL RESERVE NOTE." In other words, it's a fancy way of saying "I owe you." In other words, a glorified IOU is what the dollar is, and many other currencies in the world are also, actually. Platinum, gold, and silver are a few of the oldest currencies and valued as some of the highest currencies that exist. But—and this is a very big *but*—if you think about it, what gives them their value? People. Gold and silver are just elements, metals—essentially just "rocks"—on Planet Earth, if not for humans giving those "rocks" a certain value that is worth more or less than other rocks. If we no longer use them as actual day-to-day currency to buy and sell with, and the dollars we use do not hold the same value, then all currencies, whether paper or digital, are simply backed by the people who claim their value. Or maybe the superpowers and allies that are behind those currencies also add to the value? Hmm. OK, I am going too far in to this, and like I said, I am writing a book about it that will go much further into the world of cryptocurrency and real estate.

bit·coin
ˈbitˌkoin/

noun
a *type* of digital currency in which encryption techniques are used to regulate the generation of units of currency and verify the transfer of funds, operating independently of a central bank.

https://en.wikipedia.org/wiki/Bitcoin

As of now, this is the highest-valued cryptocurrency on the planet. So like the dollar, franc, and dinar that can be worth more or less than others, the bitcoin is worth more than all other cryptocurrencies out there. A couple of more popular ones you will hear out there in the main public are Bitcoin Cash, Ripple, Ethereum, and Litecoin. It's pretty easy to find information on those cryptos as well in Google Search and Wikipedia.

block·chain

ˈbläkˌCHān/

noun

a digital ledger in which transactions made in bitcoin or another cryptocurrency are recorded chronologically and publicly.

https://en.wikipedia.org/wiki/Bitcoin#Blockchain

This is the technology behind the currency, which creates the transaction, in order to process and be completed, establishing a recorded history of the transaction. It's almost like a bank vault of bank receipts, if you will. What does this mean for real estate? It means what has already begun actually: that cryptocurrency has already been the currency used for a buyer to purchase property with Bitcoin from a seller of a property willing to accept Bitcoin. My company's experience in these transactions has led to us starting a division and consulting firm for you to hire. Whether seller, buyer, investor, and/or real estate agent, you can hire us to oversee and guide you through the steps of the transaction to both sell the property and ensure you don't lose the deal. Here are some frequently asked questions our firm receives:

- ☐ What steps does the buyer need to take?
- ☐ What steps does the seller need to take?
- ☐ What does the buyer or seller need to know?
- ☐ What are some frequent obstacles?
- ☐ What are the tax implications?
- ☐ Are there capital gains?
- ☐ Does an escrow company or law firm play a part?
- ☐ Is it still considered a traditional purchase?
- ☐ Is it still considered a traditional sale?
- ☐ What are the risks to agent, buyer, or seller?
- ☐ What are the benefits to buyer or seller?

There are so many more facets to cryptocurrency. It really is fascinating—I don't know a better word to use. It is only going to become more popular and more mainstream. Regarding whether it is ever regulated (centralized) or controlled by "Big Brother," no one has a crystal ball. I do feel very confident in saying I do not feel it will ever be gone. Any currency can skyrocket in value and then crash in a bubble. It is still a currency used, however. Cryptocurrency will have its ups and downs, and the process of using the currency will, I am sure, continue to evolve and shift. In short, do not take this lightly or turn down business that involves crypto because you don't understand it or have little experience with it. Say yes, and reach out to us when you have a buyer or seller who has inquired with you if you can handle it, and we will guide you through the process. Look for my next book on cryptocurrency and real estate. No, that is not the title of the book. It is much cleverer than that, but it will be a secret until it's published.

At the end of the day, what I would like you to remember while reading this book is that it is not written for you to know it all at the end. It is written to make sure you know the critical aspects to this online world, and it discusses key strategies most professionals don't know about or are too lazy or complacent to use. Always be learning based and research new ways to stand above your competition. So, if you are ready, I am about to consistently reveal a series of techniques, secrets, and strategies that are going to increasingly blow your mind throughout this book as I reveal each one, and I will show you just how deep this digital online rabbit hole goes. Sound good?

NOTES

CHAPTER 2

online presence vs. present online

This is the title of one of my business summits and presentations. What do I mean by the title "online presence versus present online"? Let me use an example of being present verse having presence. Twenty years ago—actually, even ten years ago—if a small business or sales professional, say in Malibu, California, wanted to dominate the market share in his or her area, what would he or she have had to do? He or she would've needed to blanket that area with marketing, mailers, billboards, shopping carts, park benches, newspaper ads, magazine ads, and so on. This would have resulted in that person having Malibu "presence" when the rest of the competition was just "present" in Malibu. Make sense? See, most sales professionals and businesses are "present" online; however, a very small percentage have online "presence."

> RANDOM PROFESSIONAL: "Tony, I have a Facebook, LinkedIn, website, and so on. I am present online."
> ME: "Great, now how many sales did you get directly from, say, Facebook alone?"
> RANDOM PROFESSIONAL: "I closed three transactions that came directly from Facebook last year."
> ME: "Oh, so you don't do Facebook. If you did, you should have closed three transactions a week from Facebook."

You see, "present online" is merely allowing Facebook, or social media in general, to happen. Meaning, when you do get that deal or new business from social media here and there, you think to yourself, *Ahh, this must be what they are talking about with the power of social media. Now I see the importance of having Facebook and all these social network accounts.* That is only allowing it to happen because you have the accounts. It is not being purposeful or strategic in building your brand or generating business, though. I call it *lead generation versus lead assumption.* Most sales people practice lead assumption, not even realizing they are not practicing lead generation. And, by the way, lead assumption will make you a lot of money. More than likely this is the first time you have ever heard this term *lead assumption.* Why do I call it that? What's the difference? Lead assumption is putting yourself or something "out there," *assuming* it will produce a lead. For example, you might launch a direct mailer campaign, "assuming" it will produce a lead; a billboard, "assuming" it will produce a lead; going to a networking event, "assuming" it will produce a lead; sending one thousand e-mails out, "assuming" it will produce a lead; door knocking, "assuming" it will produce a lead; adding friends on Facebook or other social networks, "assuming" it will produce a lead. Lead generation, on the other hand, is simply one thing, and one thing only, to me: asking twenty people a day if they know anyone looking to buy or sell a home. This can be face to face, on the phone, text, whatever. But if you go door knocking, and the person says he or she is not interested in selling, and you turn around and walk away, or even if the person is interested in selling, that is lead assumption to me. However, if after the person says he or she is or is not interested, you go even further and ask, "Do you know anyone looking to buy or sell a home?" Well, that's high-level *lead generation.* However, lead assumption is similar to just being "present online."

"Online presence," however, is doing two things every day. I will give you ninety-eight other things to do in this book that will raise your capture rate and (ROI) return on investment even more, but if you are not doing these two things every day, those other ninety-eight things will never really work.

• • •

The First Thing...

...is having an audience that increases in size frequently. Not yearly, not monthly, not weekly, not even daily, actually—it should be increasing in size every day *throughout* the day. You added ten new friends on Facebook, ten new connections on LinkedIn, ten new people to your CRM Database...your overall audience is growing in size every day, and about twenty-five a day is a good goal to have.

• • •

The Second Thing...

...is that you give that audience valuable, relevant content consistently throughout the week, each week. Oh, and when I say "valuable content," I am not talking about boring, business-related content. I'm talking about you posting a picture of your dog doing something funny that morning, and making nine hundred complete strangers, whom you are connected with online, laugh their butts off. You see, they get value from their online connection with you. Business content is OK, too, but there is a way to do it—and many ways not to do it. We will be diving deep into these techniques throughout this book.

A question you may be asking is, why? Why is having online presence so important today and important for the future? As most people know, I primarily come from the real estate industry, both on the financing side and the sales side. This is why I frequently use examples in business and sales from my industry. Even though you may not be in real estate, the examples and strategies are the same in most industries, especially sales. That being said, here is an example of how my industry has changed, and why building an online "presence" is so important today. However, you will notice that in this particular example, it involves multiple industries.

What happened to the travel industries in the early 2000s to mid-2000s? They were annihilated for the most part, weren't they? What was the reason? A little ol' website company named...that's right, Expedia, and you probably are going to have that jingle stuck in your head now, remember? It was "Expedia...*dot commmmmmm*!" That was the first travel website of eventually a few that would rise like it. These sites would change the travel industry and the way consumers searched for best travel rates and best destinations. The main technique was that they simply gave the consumers access at their fingertips to travel information, and it was accessed easily online. As Expedia grew, and the amount of traffic and people grew online, it was easy for Expedia to approach airlines and hotels to negotiate better rates, as they were able to show those companies the amount of increasing traffic of people searching for travel rates online. Travel was officially changed forever. Some travel companies survived, though—the ones that adapted when they saw their industry changing before their eyes. They made sure that they became a resource and advertised online. I remember discussing this with a travel agent years ago. When I asked him why he thought he survived such a drastic shift in his industry, he said it brilliantly: "Tony, when Expedia launched, I looked at my career and realized that my industry had just changed forever. I, without question, better adapt. Not only should I have a website that functions just as well, I also need to embrace Expedia by becoming a resource for Expedia, and even advertise on Expedia. Don't get me wrong; it wasn't easy. I took a pay cut for quite some time as I took a step back to implement a new business model. Travel is my passion, and if I was going to survive, then I needed to sacrifice and keep moving forward and innovate. Within a couple years, I was making more than I had before. I actually owe it to Expedia—crazy, huh?"

Pretty interesting wouldn't you say? Most looked at Expedia as this giant competitor and were left in the dust, yet the ones who adapted and learned with the change survived and broke through new ceilings! Well, the founder of Expedia, I'm sure, said, "Oops, I'm sorry, I didn't mean to change your industry forever and wipe out so many old-school travel agents not willing to adapt and innovate, but now that I know I can…I think I will do it to another industry." So he decided to hop on the board of directors for another company and help them take out Blockbuster Video, which was a completely different industry. What company do you think it was? That's right, Netflix. Within months you began to see the industry change, and the traditional video stores eventually would fall. Then, as they grew and other companies like them began to launch, any company that wasn't willing to adapt sooner rather than later was failing. Fast-forward a couple of years, and what giant finally came crashing down? That's right, Blockbuster, the billion-dollar unsinkable ship. I can't help but change the lyrics in my head of that famous song, "Video killed the radio star…" to "Netflix killed the video store…" ☺ I wish I had been a fly on the wall during Blockbuster's executive board meetings when Netflix was the topic of discussion. Here is my own opinion on how these meetings may have gone:

> CSO (Chief of "Something" Officer): "Netflix!? Psssh. Don't worry, guys, we do not need to stress over Netflix. We're Blockbuster, for goodness' sake. We are unsinkable!"
>
> NEW GUY: "Are you sure? Because they sure seem to be gaining a lot of steam with consumers."

CSO: "Yes, Johnny, let me tell you why. You see, when consumers think about watching and renting a movie, they enjoy getting in their cars to drive to our Blockbuster stores, especially if they are not feeling well. Once at our stores, they love to stare at our walls of germ-covered plastic. Now this is where it really gets interesting. The consumers actually love to grab it off the wall before anyone else does, like they just won a competition. While caressing the germ-covered plastic, they then begin to read the back of it to see what the movie is about. As they read the back of the germ-covered plastic DVD, that is when we really make their day, as they see that our price tag or UPC sticker is on top of the remaining description of the movie so they can't finish reading what the movie is about or see what it is rated. This is when they decide to rent it anyway. While excited to get home to watch the movie, they sit in our checkout line with little children screaming about what kind of candy they want. (That's why we put the candy at the checkout.) You see why consumers love us now? Do you see why we don't have to worry about Netflix?"

NEW GUY: (Blink, blink) "No, I am not seeing why."

CSO: "Let me explain more of our benefits. Let's talk about the great stuff. Once they get home to watch the movie they chose of our great wall of germ-covered plastic that they couldn't finish reading about, they now, in excitement, realize that the movie is skipping because the DVD has scratches in it. Or even better, it

> skips, and the movie sucks, so it was a waste of time and money. Now, the greatest benefit to the consumer that we here at Blockbuster can give is on the next day. You will never believe it, Johnny, they actually love waking up late for work the next morning and forgetting to return the movie, so we can charge them late fees that eventually suspend their account and go to collections. This is what the consumer wants!"

Isn't it crazy to think we used to do that when we wanted to rent a movie? Feels like a hundred years ago, though. Well, I think you and I can agree that this is not what we want as consumers, is it? Of course not. What do we want? We want to be able to sign into Netflix, Apple TV, and Hulu, watch a trailer on the movie, see what others have rated the movie, press play, and if we love it, awesome. If we don't, stop playing, go to bed and move on with no worries, no hassle. What is crazy to me is that these industries changed forever simply by the consumers having access, or should I say, being given access—much like Napster changed the music industry forever. We have heard it throughout the history of sales: "Go where the people are," and the founder of Expedia and board member of Netflix did just that. He went where the people were, and where were they? Online.

Well, if you are in real estate, you may want to sit down for this next paragraph. Seriously, I really think you may want to sit down. Here's why. The founder of Expedia, who also sat on the board of Netflix, who changed those industries forever, is named Rich Barton. Sound familiar? Well, it should, because he's the founder of Zillow. I'll let you have a moment. Make sure to get a paper bag if you are feeling faint. Seriously, take all the time you need...

Breathe...

Breathe…

Are you still with me? Now, if you are *not* a real estate agent, you should probably know, this is happening in every industry. I speak and train people in various industries in the relationship and sales professions, and it is the same approach. Everything is going online, and consumers are getting access to information more and more, so the sales professionals out there who understand they need to be online and just as accessible to the consumer as the information at their fingertips will be just fine. Once consumers find the info they are looking for, you need to be easy to access to help advise them and help them get the right one. If you are, you will also grow much faster and become absolutely dominant over your competition.

So, would you say the founder of Zillow completely changed our industry? Yes, most certainly. You really want to fight this giant? Here is why that may be a very big mistake. Zillow is worth billions more than any of the national real estate brands and associations around the nation *combined*. They're not going anywhere. But here's the thing: so far this time, he's not doing the same as he did with Expedia. He's not coming to us and saying, "Hey, if somebody finds you through my platform Zillow, give them a discount. Or better yet, give me a piece." Well, not doing it yet, anyway. But the reason I don't think he's going to—or maybe he'll do it on a small level, but nothing extravagant—is this: Where does he make his billions this time? Agent advertising. Literally, it is Zillow's main profit margin. Now, if I give another agent 25 percent of my commission for a referral, why wouldn't I give Zillow a piece? If they asked for 1–5 percent of a closed transaction referral, I would pay it in a heartbeat. Maybe I just look at all this differently. Maybe I look back at history with innovations like Expedia and make sure I am ready for the same innovations to happen within real estate or any industry for that matter.

See, Zillow is not our competitor per se. It has simply given consumers access yet again to information that we used to be the gatekeepers of, the "holy land"—the Multiple Listing Service (MLS), and the MLS promised us it would never sell out. What's funny to me is how all these organizations want to rise up and take our info back from these platforms like Zillow; however, they are the reasons Zillow exists in the first place now. Do you want to know what the beginning of the end was? IDX on your website. The second the MLS allowed us as real estate agents to start having MLS on our personal websites, in real time in a cool format, was truly the beginning of the end. Why? Because the rise of predictive analytic, and data research companies was born, and anyone can pull that information now.

Consumers today do not need you to grant them access anymore. Do you know how many clients of mine, and also clients of real estate agents I coach, have had several consumers find their homes on Zillow, Trulia, and so on, and the agent wrote the offer and closed the transaction? Hundreds. Now the good thing is, real estate agents aren't going anywhere, because people need us.

Are we finding them the houses as much as we used to? Not really. But...

Are we the reason the house they see "For Sale" online is "For Sale" in the first place? Yes!

Are we still writing that outstanding cover letter? Yes!

Are we still strategic and advanced negotiators? Yes!

Do we protect them with the right disclosures so that they don't get sued? Yes!

Do we hold our buyers' hands during the process? Yes!

Do we get our sellers the right price that they were wanting? Yes!

Do we market their listings at a higher level than they could if they were just doing it on their own? Yes!

Do we beat out six other offers for our buyer? Yes!

That, by the way, is my favorite part of this job. I love it when there is low inventory because I am super competitive and want to beat out all other offers or all other agents trying to get that listing. I'm going to write that amazing cover letter. I'm going to send flowers to that seller and/or agent. Whatever I need to do, I'm going to get that deal. Bottom line, we're not going anywhere, but here's the key point of this whole revolution to our industry and all industries today: if the information is at the consumers' fingertips to find a product the second they want it, then shouldn't you be at their fingertips the second they need you to write the offer or help them buy it?

Yes!

Learn from these giants, ladies and gentlemen, because here's what's going on in our world now. If I line up one hundred homebuyers in front of all of you right now—I actually want you to picture one hundred people—all buyers who are guaranteed to be buying a house in the next ninety days here in your area, and we ask every single one:

"Do you have an agent?" And they all said, "Yes."

"Are you loyal to your agent?" And they all said, "Yes."

"Are you guaranteeing that agent will write your offer when you need it written?" And they all said, "Yes."

If we found those hundred homebuyers who are loyal to an agent and are going to have that agent write an offer on a house in the next ninety days, and we've got them all in a room, and then we asked all hundred of them: "What do you use every night before you go to bed to look at property?"

You already know the answer, don't you? Most of them would say Zillow. Some would say Trulia. Some would say Realtor.com. Some would say Redfin, and so on. Less than five out of the hundred would say, "My realtor's website, of course!" You really want to fight this? I hope not. Make sure you are embracing it. Be a premier agent for these giants online because that's where consumers go to find an agent or a home today. They're in there every day and all day, and it is where they're going to find you. Zillow is not our competitor. If anything, Zillow is my "showing specialist." How 'bout them apples? If I hear another agent tell me Zillow leads are crap, I will flip out. If you really want to know what crap is with most agents today, it is their follow-up system.

I'll challenge anybody who tells me Zillow, Trulia, Redfin, Easy Street, and Realtor.com leads are crap with a short series of questions they need to answer:

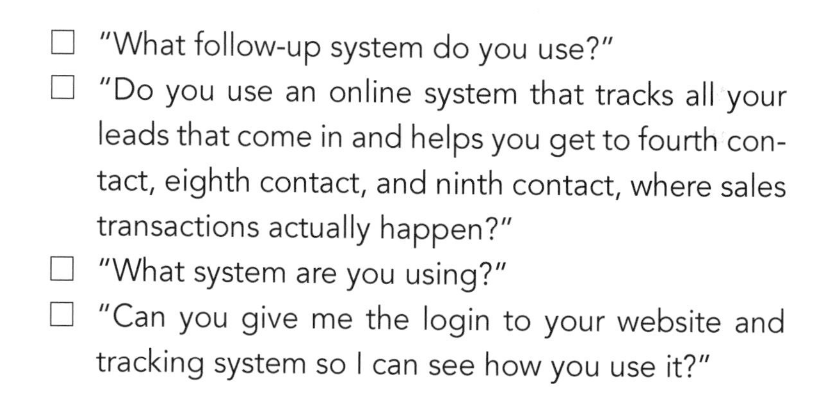

- ☐ "What follow-up system do you use?"
- ☐ "Do you use an online system that tracks all your leads that come in and helps you get to fourth contact, eighth contact, and ninth contact, where sales transactions actually happen?"
- ☐ "What system are you using?"
- ☐ "Can you give me the login to your website and tracking system so I can see how you use it?"

Now this is when I hear most agents I start to coach tell me, "All right, fine, I'm not doing it at a high level." Yes, exactly—that's why they consider Zillow leads crap. They have no follow-up system at a high level. Don't get me wrong, I get that half the leads are not qualified sometimes, or they want to rent, but what about the other half? Well, they bought a home within six months, and we unfortunately called them crap because they were at the beginning of what's called the educational phase, which on average is six to twelve months nationally. Nine months is the average. That means from the day homebuyers decide to purchase a home, nine months later, on average, they close. They start by talking with their CPA (maybe), parents, and/or company. They start using Zillow and hitting contact agents. They start going to open houses. They maybe start talking to the agents they were referred to by family or friends, and also start talking to another agent a coworker referred them to. On average, does anybody want to guess how many real estate agents, buyers talk to in their nine-month educational phase? Seventeen.

The first month they decide to buy a house, they go to fifteen open houses. That's fifteen agents right there whom they talked to, and fourteen of them had horrible tracking systems and follow-up systems that did nothing with that lead who walked into their open house. The next month they talked to a few on Zillow, and then the next month they talked to a few on Realtor.com via e-mail, phone, or whatever it was.

The unfortunate fact is, that the majority of these agents consider them crap. Why? The buyers didn't open the e-mails that they sent them with some listings on it. "Oh, I knew those people weren't serious. They didn't show up for a showing two times in a row." Why? They're at the beginning of their educational phase, probably. Still talking to their CPA, employer, financial advisor, mom and dad, or whomever. So eventually they just dwindle away from your sticky-note follow-up system, because now you're working with somebody who's actually gone under contract with you, and you've got to go do the home inspections, termite inspections, and simply just focus on that one commission check around the corner.

There is a very interesting stat out there that many don't realize, and it's that 90 percent of real estate agents are all fighting for the 10 percent of buyers buying in the next thirty days. No one is fighting for the 90 percent of all other buyers who are buying in the next six months. We're all fighting for the paycheck right now, and only 10 percent of them are buying right now.

You must have systems in place, ladies and gentlemen. You must embrace these giants and be just as accessible as the information is to people today. Zillow has also given the power back to the consumer. The more that technology and consumer-access continue to grow, the more power the consumer has. Just look at the power getting great reviews has today. Or the opposite, the extraordinary power bad reviews can have on a brand or sales person. Remember, we want everything working together to increase brand reputation and profits.

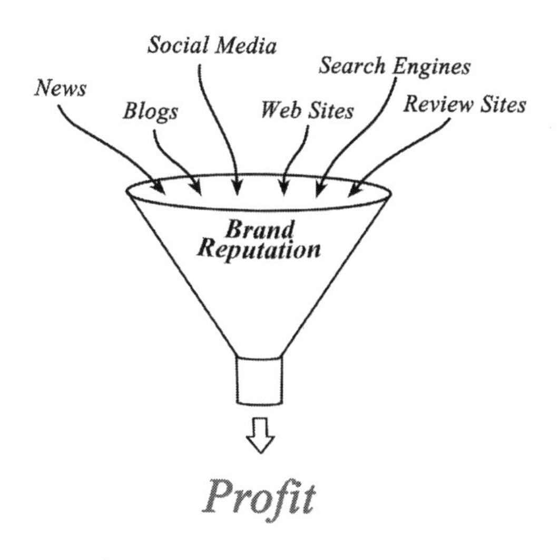

If you are not taking reviews seriously enough, you need to change that today. More and more consumers are choosing a product or service simply based on what others have said about that company or person. The younger the generation, the more common making decisions like this becomes. As a real estate agent, you should be working diligently to have your clients give you a review on at least the big platforms like Zillow, Google, YELP, etc. This will not only help you set yourself apart from your competitors but will also give you higher-quality leads. In the end, the business will come, and continue to come if you are growing your relationships and brand. Where do we do that? Online. I will coach, mentor, and teach you one hundred other techniques to use, but remember, if you are not at least doing those two things we discussed every day, there is no reason to do the other hundred techniques. So if I were to ask you, what is your online presence in your field, what would your answer be? Do you have presence? Or are you just present?

NOTES

CHAPTER 3

the "first impression" approach

www.theopulentagency.com

For the sake of this chapter, we will be discussing your real estate website. Your website is the foundation you build your entire digital presence off of. Period. It is the first impression of who you are and what you do in most sales industries. You must have a website today. Don't have one? Don't need one? Business is great without one? Or you have a basic one that gets you by, but you don't really need it because business is great? Or is business just good? Or should we say, business is just OK and paying the bills, but nothing extraordinary?

If you don't think you need a dynamic, visual website that tells your story today, try going up against a competitor of yours who does have a website that is visually dynamic. The tide is shifting, ladies and gentlemen. A client does not realize how important something is until someone educates him or her about it. That's with anything too. Don't you want to be the one who educates the other person? Now, as the majority of individual salespeople don't have visually dynamic websites that tell their stories, more than likely, neither do their competitors. So the client is left with having to choose between two or three of you based on something else. That is, until a new competitor arrives on the scene with a powerful visual website—and doesn't just show the client the site but also how the site is used to benefit him or her as the client.

Wait, did I just say, "show the client the site"? Most times today, the consumer has already researched and looked at it. How about when a new competitor arrives on the scene, and the potential client you are both fighting for Googled the competitor after seeing his or her name or advertisement and comes across his or her website?

Then the client Googles the "other guy" and looks at his or her site. What's the client's first impression now? Who is looking more successful? Who seems to be more experienced than the other? See, today, the website is the first impression. Now more than ever, actually. Why? Well, today, information is at the client's, and consumer's fingertips. It is easier today to look at a website on the go than it was even just a few years ago. It's not just important to have a website today; it's critical.

THE MODERN-DAY FIRST IMPRESSION

Let's talk about first impressions for a couple minutes. What was the moment of the "first impression" before the Internet became a way of life? When did the client first see it? Depending on the industry, it could have been when he or she met you and saw how you were dressed. In some industries, it was the car you pulled up in. Based on what a client saw, he or she would immediately have a perception of your success or lack of success, or a perception of your experience, or lack of experience.

I want you to follow me on this next example. Let's say years ago, before the Internet, a consumer is given the name of a real estate agent to call to list his or her home for sale. Another friend also refers the consumer to a different real estate agent. The consumer can't Google either one, because there is no Google. The day he or she sets the appointment for each agent to come to the house, they simply speak on the phone. Not really a first impression. Both could sound great on a call. One could sound more experienced, I guess, but the real first impression is going to happen...when? That's right, when both agents pull up in front of the client's home. What will that first impression be? You guessed it—the car. First agent pulls up in front of the client's gorgeous home in an old, used car, with an advertising magnet on the car door that states "I sell well," one hubcap missing on the wheel, and an exhaust pipe that backfires as the agent turns off the engine. Second agent, a few hours later, pulls up in front of the client's gorgeous home in a 5 Series BMW. What is the first thought in the client's mind when comparing the first impressions? One agent is successful; the other is not as successful. That agent must have sold more than the other agent. Or that agent is more experienced, and the other is less experienced. Even if the client is wrong, perception is what? *Reality*. Even if the first agent is a more qualified agent to sell the home, that agent is now, having to make up for the first impression. That agent is already starting in second place right out of the gate.

Well, today, ladies and gentlemen, clients no longer have to wait for us to show up before they have their "first impression" of who we are. Today, the moment potential clients are referred to us, they Google us; and what's on the first page of Google when they Google us? Our websites—I hope. It better be on the first page of Google when somebody Googles your first and last name. SEO (search engine optimization) is critical to have today. Once consumers look at your website, guess what? They do exactly what you do when you look at your own website. If you look at your website and think to yourself, "Wow!" then consumers look at your website and say the same thing. But if you look at your website and think to yourself, "Eh? I mean, it's what's provided to me from my company, so I really don't have a choice." Then just know that consumers look at your site and think, "Eh!" I saw a stat that showed 68 percent of consumers Google us before picking up the phone. That stat continues to rise more and more every day and is already high at 68 percent! Oh, and what did I say—the client "Googles" you, not "Yahoos" you. So where you show on Google results is key. We will discuss that in a few chapters.

If we know we are Googled when a client is given our name, I only ask you this: Are clients impressed at what they see? Are you proud of what they see? I had a friend of mine once tell me, "Well, I get calls all the time, so I guess they like what they see, and my business is doing great." I asked him, "How do you know they have all called you? Are you confident everyone is impressed with what they see?" He added, "Well, Tony, you're assuming that people haven't called me based on what they saw when they looked me up." Yes, and you're assuming they all have. Which is worse? See, I am going to impress them at such a high level that I know I have done everything I can to hook any client who looks me up. I am not going to assume it's decent enough, and I am sure they will still call me. See, websites are the modern-day first impression. They are the modern-day "car," if you will. Here is another way to look at it.

DISCLAIMER: Now, I have to choose my next words very wisely for my national real estate brand CEO friends reading this. But follow me on this for any industry. I am sure my national real estate brand friends will catch on, as they will understand where I am going with this. I have no idea why my font size has shrunk. Must be a glitch. ☺

If we now see the reality of the modern-day first impression being a website and digital identity, whereas the first impression years ago was the car you drove, I only ask you this: If you worked years ago for a national or international retail brand as a field sales rep, in any industry, and that company "*provided*" you a company "car" to be able to get from A to Z and do your job, what kind of car was it? Basic, right? Simple technology. Economical. Oh, and what do all the other sales reps (your competitors) with your same company have as well? They all have the exact same company car. You wouldn't really be rising above the competition at this point, would you? Sound familiar? Is what's provided to us for no cost ever really spectacular? I'm curious, though, what you think would happen if you went to the owner of your company that's provided you a company car for your first impression to hit the field in, and you asked them this:

> SALES REP: "Thank you very much for the company car. I really do appreciate it, but I was wondering, is this the kind of car you drive?"

COMPANY OWNER: "Uhh, no. [Laughing] No, you see, we have a 7 Series BMW. See how it has more pages, tabs, and functions...I mean horsepower, engineering, and leather. No, ours costs thousands more to build, I mean buy. We provide you the basic to do your job."

SALES REP: "Well, I appreciate that, but I want to go after the big boys. I want to go after the big clients out there, and I don't want to pull up in the same car that our other ten thousand reps have nationally, and even the five locally who have been calling on those same big clients. I want to pull up in front of that business or house, and I want them to walk out and see my first impression and think to themselves, 'Oh, this must be the number-one salesperson with the company.'"

COMPANY OWNER: "Well, I appreciate your tenacity, Tony, but if you want my 7 Series BMW, you need to go do that yourself. We provide you the basics to do your job. But don't worry, Tony, every few years or so, when you've put a lot of miles on that company car, we're going to go ahead and replace that car with a newer version that this time has a little more custom pages and functions, I mean shiny wheels and leather, and you'll be excited to go into the field again because it's newer, and it's got Bluetooth now."

Still following me?

Good, because I wasn't going to look like ninety thousand other real estate agents, or a million other agents, for that matter. I wanted to look like the top 1 percent of real estate agents. This next statement might hurt a little bit, but it is my strong opinion. Websites or technology that are provided to agents for hanging their license at a certain company, are almost always for the bottom 80 percent in production. The top 1 percent, however, rarely have or use what is provided to them. They go out and build and brand themselves at a much higher level. Why? They want to rise above their competition. I remember a conversation with this other rookie agent I was in a class with.

AGENT: "Why are you researching the top one percent of agents, Tony?"
ME: "Because that is my competition, and I need to do what they do."
AGENT: "Uh, Tony, I hate to break it to you, but the top one percent is not your competition. They also definitely don't think you are their competition."
ME: "That's where you and I are extremely different. They are my competition, actually, because I have no desire to compete with the bottom eighty percent. I have no desire to compete with the bottom ninety percent, for that matter."

So I risked it all. Literally. With every dollar and coin to my name at that moment, I launched an extraordinary website. This would prove to be absolutely game changing very, very quickly. It was, without question, the first key to my success. Let's now discuss what the modern-day first impression should have for the best opportunity for growth.

PRIMARY NEUTRAL DOMAIN

When launching a website, you first want to make sure you have a primary neutral domain. Example, www.theopulentagency.com, which is my real estate website. Does it say the Opulent Agency Malibu? No. My main site is not area specific; it's neutral. Be careful with these area-specific domains, or you'll find yourself wondering why you're not broadening your brand or why you don't get referral fees at a high level. In my first book, I said my goal wasn't to just make one million in gross commission as an agent. My real true goal had derived from that great saying we've heard for decades:

> *"I'd rather have 1 percent of a hundred men's efforts than 100 percent of my own."*

Well, in real estate, it's not 1 percent, it's 25 percent, and...

> *"I would rather have 25 percent of a hundred agents' efforts globally than 100 percent of my own locally."*

I wanted one hundred referral fees nationally and internationally. How would I do this? By thinking broad and not narrow minded. Because I stay neutral in my marketing, both locally and online, when somebody who maybe is from out of the area comes across me, or my site, he or she can't see if I am only in one city or area. So he or she still calls. Well, I want that phone call. I want the person to contact me on my site or networks. I want the random consumer or seller in Palm Springs, California, who came across my website because one of his friends clicked on it—you see what your friends are clicking on Facebook—and then he sees my site and still calls me to ask:

> CUSTOMER: "Hello, Tony, I see that your headquarters are based in LA, but you sell everywhere. Do you cover Palm Springs?"
> ME: "No, I don't cover PS."

But now what do I get? You got it, a 25 percent referral fee. Or I may cover that area and say, "Yes!" and I'll launch my brand in Palm Springs right then and there and partner with a local agent who knows the market and will do all the local groundwork while I do all the marketing and advertising, especially if it's a multimillion-dollar home in Palm Springs. Or Chicago, or New York, or Costa Rica. No limits.

Here's an example: I had an agent from Calabasas, California, call me who wanted to start coaching with me, and she said, "I'm having a hard time being able to get the Malibu market up and running. Like, I want to break into the Malibu market, but it's not going well for some reason. I can't seem to get any business or listings."

And I said to her: "OK, well, let's work on this together. Send me all of your links—your website, your Facebook, your Yelp, your Zillow, everything you have online, send it to me." The first URL she sends me—it's not this, but it's like this; I'm not going to give you her real website—ISellCalabasas.com. I said, "Coaching session over. ☺ What on Earth makes you think that a seller in Malibu would want to list their home with an agent who has a website called I sell Calabasas dot com?"

She tells me, "Tony, the two towns are next door to each other. I'm sure they know I know both areas." I couldn't help but tell her how mistaken she was. Horrible assumption on her part—horrible, because as far as those homeowners in Malibu are concerned, where is she the expert? Exactly. Calabasas.

I went on to tell her, "That's why you're not breaking into the Malibu market. Your business card says Calabasas, your flyers say Calabasas, your marketing says Calabasas, the signature line on your e-mails says Calabasas." We must be careful to avoid being too narrow in our area-specific branding, especially if we would love to grow our business.

Now don't get me wrong. I have dozens of area-specific domains. I have domains with the city names of San Diego, Del Mar, Cornado, Santa Barbara Montecito, Ventura Beach, Malibu, Palisades, Santa Monica, Beverly Hills, Brentwood, Hollywood Hills, Westwood, Bel Air, Manhattan Beach, and many more. Now that I am expanding our brand across the globe, I have domains for Boston, Miami, Atlanta, New York, Chicago, and Seattle, along with domains with the names of states like California, Hawaii, New York, Texas, and Florida. The reason I have these area-specific domains is so when I'm marketing one of those areas—take, for instance, my own town in Los Angeles in

Brentwood—and I send out www.TheBrentwoodLifestyle.com, which is our custom URL for Brentwood when I'm targeting only the residents of Brentwood, and they click on it, where do you think it takes them? That's right. It redirects them to www.TheOpulentAgency.com. They don't care that when they clicked on one URL, it took them to another. They clicked on www.TheBrentwoodLifestyle.com, which means as far as that resident of Brentwood is concerned, the Opulent Agency is an expert where? Brentwood. However, all my primary marketing, like business cards, signature lines on e-mails, and so on, is going to just say www.TheOpulentAgency.com so I can stay broad in my branding and have a larger pool of potential business and either handle it myself, or at least now get the call to refer it out, and get what again? That's right: 25 percent, baby!

PROPERTY SEARCH

The modern-day website has property search. I just know nobody is using it. What are they using today? I know you don't want to admit it, but let it out. There you go—yes, Zillow. It is a *fact*. Now, I know we talked about Zillow earlier, and there is no question that Zillow, along with platforms like it, have changed our industry forever. But Zillow is not the end of the real estate agent, as so many seem to be afraid of. No, Zillow is the end of the MLS as we know it. See, the MLS is the agent's MLS. What do you already know is the consumer's MLS? Yes, Zillow. If agents want to challenge me on this, I will ask them to give me the login and password to the back end of their website. I will then ask them to pull up their website analytics, and I will show most agents that out of the three hundred people who visited their website last month, fewer than twenty of them clicked on their property search page. Out of the twenty who actually did click on the property search tab, sixteen had an 89 percent "bounce rate," which means the second they clicked on it, they left it. They're not using real estate agent websites to search for property anymore; that was fifteen years ago. They don't need that anymore. They have a dozen real estate search platforms to use that offer twenty times the information the archaic MLS ever will. I know you know this. For every ten producing agents I ask the following question to, seven to eight now raise their hands:

> How many of you are dealing with buyers right now, and every time you send them MLS e-mails and links, the buyers text you back Zillow, Trulia, and Redfin links of homes they are interested in?

There is an ever-increasing percentage of agents who are experiencing this every day. You might be one of them. So what are consumers really using our websites for? Why do they need our websites? More importantly, why do you need a website today? Because websites get listings. That's why. And last I checked, listings are king. Listings are king and queen of surviving any market downturn. A "shift," right? These are the techniques that help you become "shift proof." Buyers' agents are the first to go in a shift. Consumers are using our websites today to see, "Is this agent reputable enough to list my house for sale? Is he or she worth ninety minutes in our living room to interview? Does this agent know how to market him- or herself before I trust him or her to market my home?" That's what they're looking at today, and guess what: they will probably never go to your website ever again. I track it every few months. I text ten of my past clients from about two and a half years ago, and with nine out of the ten, it usually goes something like this:

> ME: "I'm curious, I'm just taking a quick poll. When is the last time you went to my website?"
> CLIENT: "Two and a half years ago when you were selling our house. Why would I go to your website since?"
> ME: "I don't know, to see what's happening in your neighborhood. Just-solds. Look at property on MLS. Read my bio, watch my videos, you know, just surf around in its awesomeness."
> CLIENT: "I have Zillow for that, Tony, and your newsletter that you send me once a month from your CRM that says what has happened in the market or my neighborhood."

See, my website's main purpose, then and still today, was to get me the appointment, and then I could get the listing and sell the house. Now if you go to my website, you will see a tab that says "Property Search." Want to guess what happens when you click on it? Go for it. Seriously, take a break real quick and go to www.theopulentagency.com and click "Property Search." I dare you. ☺

Did you? Pretty shocking, right? Is it, though? Or is what you just saw on my website simply common sense?

AN INTERNATIONAL FIRST IMPRESSION

I am primarily a high-end luxury real estate agent. Although we handle all levels of clientele, for this example I am going to share a fact about luxury real estate. What do wealthy people who own high-end properties have in their bank accounts? Yes, usually money. What news do you think they watch all week, then? They are without question watching the financial and world news channels. While they are watching these networks all week, anytime they hear the reporter mention anything about the US housing market, what words do you think they hear the reporter say? Almost always at some point, the reporter, while discussing housing in America, will mention that foreign money is pouring in to America's real estate markets and international buyers moving assets to America's housing market. What do you think this high-end homeowner is going to ask you when it comes to possibly listing and marketing his or her home for sale? "What is your global reach? What is your international branding? How are you planning on marketing my property outside of California, outside the United States and overseas globally?"

Why? Because they hear about it all the time. These are wealthy and/or business-savvy people. They hear CNBC, Bloomberg, and CNN talking about foreign money pouring into America all the time. So it's important to them that you know how to capture or take advantage of this international market. When potential clients are researching me online and reviewing my website, they can see we are international. It feels international. Our website has a series of international flags at the top that gives the site the ability to switch to multiple foreign languages, making it easy for a foreign national to review our website and listings as well. These techniques that I integrated into my online and digital presence would not only show my sellers I was the better choice, it actually led to me getting international listings all over the world too.

In 2010 and 2011, I started to explode with international listings in Costa Rica, Panama, Brazil, Romania, Canada, Paris France, Russia, Japan, all because of the techniques I'm teaching here. Building relationships with people all over the world. Adding international diplomats and business owners as friends on Facebook. They would see the level of marketing I would do on my own local listings in Los Angeles, and it led them to reach out and ask almost the exact same question every time: "Can you help us market our listing out here?"

That then led me to friend request foreign real estate agents, from all over the world on Facebook, and connect with them on Linkedin as well. These same techniques also led to getting listings all over the United States and bringing on partner associates in different major cities who would be the local agents on the listing there, and I would be handling all the marketing of the property. This is why almost every day now, I am asked by agents all over the nation to help them market and sell properties. Oh, and don't for a second think this has anything to do with me just being lucky, or because of my being on the show *Million Dollar Listing*, or because of being a speaker, or because of writing my first book, or because I lived in Beverly Hills or something. After the 2009 economic crash, I was living in a little town an hour north of Malibu called Ventura, California. I had my little apartment and was struggling for two or three years while building relationships online, both locally and globally, that would end up resulting to this success. It doesn't matter where you're from. Don't forget that. I said it in my first book:

"Forget farming a neighborhood; I'm farming Earth."

Just as I said about having 25 percent of a hundred agents' efforts globally rather than 100 percent of my own locally, my goal in 2010 was to achieve one hundred referral fees or marketing fees out of the state of California and all over the world. Since then I have helped market and sell well over a billion in volume globally. I can't stress this enough to you: think global, not just local.

FIRST IMPRESSION—SOCIAL PRESENCE

The modern-day website has a spectacular social presence, meaning your social media is present on the site. Ninety-nine percent of websites in the world, and especially in the United States, have what social buttons on their homepage? Facebook, Twitter, YouTube, Google, Instagram, Pinterest, Snapchat...and when you click on the website's Facebook or social network button, where do you go? Exactly, you go to facebook.com. Congratulations, "Welcome to my website, now leave it." Not exactly helping people to stay on the website, are they? Yet, that is 99 percent of websites in America. But if you go to my website, you won't see the traditional social media presence with home page social buttons you click on and leave my site. Well, that is because the people who built my website are geniuses, and they figured out how to reverse the social website platform. When you are on the home page of my website, www.theopulentagency.com, I only have a tab that says "Social," and when you click that tab, all of my individual posts from every social network I have come feeding into my website, creating their own live interactive news feed, as if it is my own social network.

(http://www.theopulentagency.com/social)

That means every time I post anything on any social network of mine, the SEO of my website is firing with new content and new data, which Google loves more than anything. This website company is genius. Its platform is unlike anything you've seen before, because it's not your

WordPress or your semicustom template websites like so many have. The company builds its sites with its own code, almost like a social network. For those who don't know what a social network is built off of, it's built off of genius students at Harvard years ago who knew how to create a new language online called code, to put this simply, which created a two-way interactive live website where people could communicate live. Still today, these social media giants are just writing more and more code. Every time they roll out a new feature on Facebook, it's because they wrote more code to create the new feature. Same with Instagram or any other social network—they're writing more code to create new features.

THE MOBILE FIRST IMPRESSION

Here's a big problem I see across all industries right now. On the very few small business or sales professional desktop websites that I am impressed with, when I go to their website from my phone, all the impressiveness goes out the door. Words are not aligned correctly, margins are in weird spots, it's hard to find the menu button, the design of the mobile version doesn't match the design of the desktop site, and so on. Making sure your website company is taking the time to build you an outstanding mobile version to your site is critical. Why? Because online activity is shifting right now, and in the coming years, the traffic to your website coming from a mobile device will only continue to increase—as it drastically has already over the last couple of years.

Mobile is going to surpass desktop, and eventually the desktop will be dead. It's just where it's going. I can count the devices every time I speak, whether it's a hall of ten thousand people or a room of fifty people, and more and more of the desktops/laptops are disappearing. Now laptops will far outlast your traditional desktops that are left out there; however, eventually the tablets will start to do everything that the laptops can do. Or the 2-in-1 laptops we see these days, where the laptop can separate the screen and keyboard, making it a tablet. Technology will just continue to evolve and have more and more mobile ability. This means that most people are going to be looking at your online presence and media from their phones. Will your presence still look impressive to them?

THE DEATH OF E-MAIL

What about communication? How do people want to communicate? E-mail? No, most do not want to communicate via e-mail. The only people who think e-mail is the right way and preferred way to communicate are the people who have an AOL e-mail address. If you in fact have an AOL e-mail still, sorry, not sorry. As you will see throughout this book, texting / instant messaging and social media messaging are the main ways people communicate today. They are the preferred ways to communicate. How do we evolve with these levels of communication within our website today? If a prospect or client visits my website or most websites today and wants to contact the company, he or she clicks "Contact Us" and fills out the little e-mail pop-up, so someone responds to them, usually within the next twenty-four hours. The larger the company today, the harder they make it to find that "Contact Us" tab too. They have also become brilliant at covering almost every possible question in the FAQs or Help section of the site. This is not just because they are trying to keep costs down on staff that take calls. The main reason this has grown in popularity is because of us, consumers—consumers who don't have the time to make a call or wait for a response. The consumers who also definitely don't have the time to wait on hold for twenty-seven minutes listening to Lionel Richie's Greatest Hits. The younger the consumer, the less time he or she has to communicate or research.

This is where *live chat* has really exploded in popularity and effectiveness the last couple years. You have probably seen it right? You visit a website, and a little chat box pops up in case you want to ask a question and get answers or resolution faster. If it's true 24/7 live chat, even better. This level of communication continues to evolve, and in many cases live chat on a website is now being powered by artificial intelligence that has been designed and developed to answer questions just like a human being would have answered it. A term that is also gaining popularity is the word "bots." Bots in my opinion are an example of artificial intelligence where you create a message response system for the most frequently asked questions your business or website gets asked, and it can make it look like you personally and quickly responded to them. Now that's service! There is much to learn about AI and technology like bots, so as I always say, when you want to learn more, *ask YouTube*.

WHAT'S BEHIND THE CURTAIN?

If you think my front end on this modern-day first impression is impressive, wait until you see how the back end of the website is built. This is where *many* website design companies or do-it-yourself website platforms are a horrible choice. The key to a great website and increasing your organic SEO is having a very well-built back end. This is where many professionals get stiffed by website companies. The site is doing nothing for the professional, but it looks great on the front end.

The back end of the company that built my site is nothing short of brilliance. First, their AI editor has been in place long before all these companies today saying they have artificial intelligence technology in their systems. I swear, all I hear today is AI, AI, AI, just to be trendy. Yet, most companies' AI doesn't even work well. The company that built my site had it way before most. They make it so simple to edit the back end of your website. It literally is the same way we edit on a social media network. They also know how to attach the right keywords and phrases on the back end to help with SEO. The website has its own social media management system built on the back end as well. This allows me to post on a few platforms from my website instead of having to go to each network or use a third-party management system. Everywhere I turn, this company stands above all others and only continues to find new and innovative ways to dominate—and every month it seems. So, are you ready for your own modern-day makeover? Let's do it.

YOUR FIRST-IMPRESSION MAKEOVER

My passion is to help people more than it is to sell homes. I love to give value, and am going to give you great value right now. I also am trying to not get blasted with e-mails by ten thousand people who read this book and ask me, "Who built your website, Tony?" So, I'm going to get that out of the way here.

The company that builds my websites is named Mopro. Their website is www.mopro.com. (Promo: VIPAgent) It is an incredible company, as I am sure you've read in this chapter or have seen on my sites already. However, I'm going to give you the same amazing gift I was given. I found Mopro through a friend of mine named Brian, and he showed me this spectacular hair salon website and said, "Check this website out, Tony." (No, not because I need a hair salon. Don't make fun of me. ☺) I clicked on the site and immediately saw such a difference between it and most websites out there. I couldn't believe the way it looked and functioned. I called Mopro that minute and started the process of building a website with them. I was extremely impressed with the company and its platform. Especially their own slogan, *"the death of DIY"* (Do It

Yourself) Want to see me smash a brand new MAC with a shovel? Here you go,

https://youtu.be/qureTMhUxCo

I like most people would rather rub my grandmothers feet, than have to build a *great* custom website myself, and "great" being the operative word.

Needless to say, Mopro's websites and the way they build them should cost thousands of dollars, and many people have paid that. My friend knew some people high up, though, and he gave me a promo code. The code I was given gave me a massive discount. Normally the websites are not cheap to build and launch. In addition to that, Mopro's hosting was $299 a month with a two-year minimum commitment and contract. The promo video that they shoot for customers who launch websites was $5,500. All professionals should have this. It's like a TV commercial of who you are, your team, your brand, your areas, and more. Mopro actually sends the videography team to you to shoot it. Well, are you ready for the same amazing deal I get? I will say the promo code has changed over the last couple years, but the executives at Mopro have given me permission to give all of you in this book a promo code that will always work as long as they are still there. Here is what it also will give you:

PROMO CODE: VIPAgent (All Industries)
BUILD OUT: No Cost
LAUNCH: No Cost
CONTRACT: Month to Month—No Contract
HOSTING: $149 instead of $299
PROMO VIDEO: $1,500 instead of $5,500—and very important, you don't have to shoot a video. That is just the discounted price if you choose to.

In other words, you're welcome. ☺ Because I just gave you the "Rolls Royce" of a "Modern-Day First Impression" for only $149 a month. Personally, on my sites, I have paid some additional costs to have some great video content and features. But overall, you are getting everything Mopro has to offer with that promo code. Even Google has a partnership with Mopro, where Google refers customers and small businesses to Mopro because of how impressed Google has been with the platform and technology of Mopro.

NOTES

CHAPTER 4

the "social" approach

www.facebook.com/giordano.global

In this chapter, we are not talking about the Facebook business page here, so do not think of anything that has to do with your business page right now; only think of your Facebook friend page for this chapter.

We will discuss your business page in chapter 11. What is the social approach to online networking? It is exactly that. Social. It can easily be compared to years and years ago, going to a social gathering where your friends and family told you to get off your phone and socialize. Be in the moment, make them laugh, care what they have to say, and enjoy their company. Here's the odd thing: we have to socialize the same way online as well. They don't care about your business when it comes to social networking. They want to get to know *you*. It is not just about what you have to share either; it is about making sure you interact with your audience, your online friends and connections, as if you are actually sitting face-to-face with them. Let me say that again: the approach to social networking and building relationships online is pretending you are sitting face-to-face with them. What do I mean by that?

> "A digital relationship is one hundred times more powerful than a real-life relationship in the same period of time..."
> — #TonyG

Now, you may be asking yourself, "What on earth are you talking about, Tony? You're telling me—just so I'm clear—that somebody I'm friends with on Facebook, named, let's say, Jane, whom I've never met face to face and only have a digital relationship with, is one hundred times more bonded and powerful of a relationship than someone I actually have in my life whom I talk to every day?" Yes, that is exactly what I am saying. Here is the key to this statement of mine, though: the last six words, **"in the same period of time"**—that's the key. Here is what I mean by this.

SCENARIO ONE

Let's go back in time. Say I walk into a Starbucks twenty years ago. I see a friend of mine named John talking to a total stranger. I walk up to John and say hi.

> JOHN: "Tony, oh my goodness, what a coincidence. This is Jennifer. Jennifer, this is Tony. Tony is a real estate agent. Tony, Jennifer is going to be buying a home soon. You two should talk."
> ME: "Oh, nice to meet you, Jennifer."
> JENNIFER: "Yeah, I'm probably two or three months away from buying."

She's in the middle of her educational phase, maybe. Or she still needs to get her finances in order. We exchange information. She tells me what she's kind of looking for, and then that's it. Maybe we continue talking to John, and then eventually, after my coffee is ready, I say my good-byes and head out the door. Remember, this example is twenty years ago. I go out to my car, drive back to the office, sit at my desk, grab my little sticky-note pad, write, "Call Jennifer tomorrow morning," and slap it on my computer. Or maybe Outlook Express is new and exciting, lol, and I put a little bell reminder in my calendar to follow up with her. Next day, "PING!" Along with that, she just went home and threw my business card on the counter, and later the card will more than likely disappear in to the trash can. So the next day I call her to check in.

JENNIFER: "Oh, thanks for reaching out. So here's what I'm looking for. But as I said, I am still a couple months away from buying. Still figuring things out."
ME: "Great. Would you like me to send you some listings that fit your criteria?"
JENNIFER: "Sure, Tony, you can send me some listings. I'll let you know if I want to see any."

A few more days go by. I haven't heard from her.

ME: "Hey, just checking in. Did you want to see any of the properties I have sent you?"
JENNIFER: "No, but keep sending them my way."

So I send some more, just like the other two agents that are sending her listings whom she spoke to before she ever met me. A few more days go by; maybe I do another follow-up. Bottom line, in the three weeks that I have been working with her, how much does Jennifer know about me? This is a real-life, face-to-face relationship too. How close are we (twenty years ago) after only knowing each other for three weeks? How much does Jennifer know about me? How much do I know about her?

Nothing, really. Right? I'm the real estate agent trying to capture her business, and we have a mutual friend named John. I'm one afternoon away from her walking into a Sunday open house by herself—you know where this is going—and befriending the listing agent who is holding the house open and having this conversation:

LISTING AGENT (used-car salesman voice): "You know, Jennifer, you could get a better deal if you use me, because I can represent both sides and offer a discounted commission to my seller and get you a better price."
JENNIFER THINKS: *Well, I don't really know that guy Tony anyway.*

This scenario still happens to this day, and every day. All of a sudden, Jennifer is no longer opening my e-mails. She stops returning my phone calls and texts. Days go by. Jennifer has gone completely MIA (missing in action). This leads me to call who, to find out what's going on with her? You guessed it, our friend John, who introduced me to Jennifer at Starbucks, of course.

ME: "John, have you heard from Jennifer? She's kind of gone MIA."
JOHN: "You haven't heard? I thought you knew, Tony. She bought a house, bro."
ME: "No, I did not hear that."

JOHN: "Ah, Tony, sorry about that...yeah, I guess sometimes it's better to represent both sides, and it's a better deal for the buyer or something. I'm sure you've done that, Tony."
ME: "Hmm, yeah. Well, tell Jennifer I said hello."

As I said, this scenario happens every day to salespeople. Now enter Exhibit A, the Digital Relationship.

SCENARIO TWO

Let's use the same exact example, actually. I walk into Starbucks, I see a friend of mine named John talking to a total stranger. I walk up to John.

JOHN: "Tony, oh my goodness, what a coincidence. This is Jennifer. Jennifer, this is Tony. Tony is a real estate agent. Tony, Jennifer is going to be buying a home soon. You two should talk."
ME: "Oh, nice to meet you, Jennifer."
JENNIFER: "Yeah, I'm probably two or three months away from buying."

We exchange information and say our good-byes, but this time I'm not slapping the sticky note on my computer back at the office. I'm not waiting till my calendar "pings" me the next day to follow up. See, this time, within an hour of meeting her at Starbucks, I open up Facebook and go to my friend John's account and open his friend list. I scroll down his friend list to the J's in his friends list; there are three Jennifers he's friends with, and there's the Jennifer I just met. I click "add friend." This is within an hour of meeting her, not days later. I sent her a request within the hour.

WHEN THE LEAD IS BOILING HOT

Tony Giordano has sent you a friend request, and what does Jennifer do? She accepts it. Why? She just met me—that's why she accepts my friend request. See, the "pressure," if you will, or level of obligation that someone has to accept a friend request is at the highest point it ever will be right after meeting someone new. And every hour that goes by after I meet her that I don't send a friend request, the amount of obligation and pressure to accept drops way down. So of course she accepts my friend request. Now in three weeks, how much does Jennifer know about me? Everything. Except for our dark secrets. Don't share those! We all have them; nobody needs to know about them. ☺ Upon accepting my friend request, she sees that we have eight mutual friends. One of those mutual friends on Facebook is her best friend named Amy.

> JENNIFER: "Amy, how do you know this guy Tony Giordano who John just introduced me to at Starbucks?"
> AMY: "Oh, Tony is great. We'll buy a house from him one day. He's super friendly too. Funny thing, both of you have a dog named Roxy."

JENNIFER: "Oh, that's cool. OK, well, see you next week on girls' night."

A couple days go by, and the Chicago Bulls are in town, playing the Lakers. I go on Facebook and post how the Bulls beat the Lakers because I'm a diehard Bulls fan, and little do I know that Jennifer's a diehard Bulls fan, too, and she lived in Chicago most of her life. So Jennifer, of course, comments on my post about the Bulls.

JENNIFER COMMENT: "You're a Bulls fan, Tony? I grew up in Chicago. I love the Bulls!"
MY COMMENT REPLY: "No way, so great. What a game last night, right?"
JENNIFER'S COMMENT REPLY: "Yeah, what a game. Let's catch a game next time."

Couple more days go by, and she sees in her news feed on Facebook a photo with a big red bow on the front door of a cute little house with this young couple standing in front of it who just bought it and tagged me in the photo because they were my clients. The post reads: "Thanks for finding us our perfect dream home, Tony."

Jennifer starts to picture herself standing in front of her new home with a big red bow on the front door when I do that same post for her. As days go by, she's also seen me post some content related to real estate and has commented or asked a question. Next morning I wake up, first task of the day, turn off alarm, grab my phone, and open my Facebook like the morning paper (I know you do too), and guess whose birthday it is? Jennifer's.

POST TO HER TIME LINE: "Happy birthday, Jennifer. Hopefully I can get you that 'birthday gift' soon. You know what I'm talking about. Wink wink. ☺"
JENNIFER COMMENT: "Thanks. Tony. Some of my friends and I are all going out tonight. If you're not doing anything, feel free to stop by. We're having a little party at Mastros Steakhouse. Otherwise, talk to you soon, and yes, hopefully you can give me that 'birthday gift' soon, wink wink. ☺"

Now in three weeks, she walks into a Sunday afternoon open house by herself, because we all have buyers who do it. You will never get them to stop. They see an open house sign, they're going in with or without you. Here's the thing, though, I don't mind that she goes by herself, because now she walks up and starts talking to the listing agent, and the listing agent says once again, just like in scenario one:

LISTING AGENT (used car-salesmen voice) "You know, Jennifer, you could get a better deal if you use me, because I can represent both sides and offer a discounted commission to my seller and get you a better price. "

But now what does Jennifer say?

JENNIFER: "Sorry, I have an agent. I'm just looking."

Why was there such a shift from scenario one to scenario two? Why didn't she take the listing agent's offer to use him? Because she's human; that's why she still uses me. Humans have something called guilt, and right at that point when she's being pitched to bail on me, she has this little white angel appear on her shoulder who whispers in her ear.

ANGEL ON HER SHOULDER: "Psst, Jennifer, you know you can't post on Facebook that you just bought a new house and let Tony see that. It will crush him. He's your friend. He just said happy birthday to you the other day…wink wink. ☺"

Facebook took our six degrees of separation, pulled us together, and built a strong bond between us in a fraction of the time it would have taken to get to know each other in any other way. How long would I have had to know Jennifer, before there was a Facebook, to learn that much about her, which I've now learned in just weeks and even in hours on Facebook? Anybody want to guess? At least a couple of years, right? Think about it. Before Facebook, I would have had to first gain her as a client to learn more about her over the month or two I showed her homes and located one for her. However, before Facebook, I may have not even locked her in as a client, as scenario one showed. A few more months would have to go by, and we'd have to be at the same beach walking our dogs at the same time and start talking to only then realize that both of our dogs are named Roxy. Of course, at that moment is where she probably finally says, "By the way, Tony, sorry I didn't use you as my agent. It just made more sense to use the listing agent because I got a better deal." (Even though that's just a pitch.) More months would go by, and one night I walk in to a restaurant and see her sitting at the bar with my friend Amy, walk up to both of them, and say, "Hey, how do you two know each other?" only to learn they are best friends. Oh, and come to find out, the three of us just happen to be going to the same game that night, Bulls versus Lakers, where Jennifer tells me she's a die-hard Bulls fan. Of course, before Facebook, we were left to say, "This is crazy, what a small world." That's where that stupid saying came from, because we didn't know how small the world really was until something like that happened.

Now we know it's not just small; Facebook has shown us that it's microscopic. After I walk away from them sitting at the bar, little do I know Jennifer looks at Amy and says:

> JENNIFER: "I feel so bad. My friend John introduced me to him about a year ago when I was getting ready to buy my house, but I ended up using a different agent. I had no idea we had so much in common."

AMY: "I wish I had known when you were looking, because I totally would have told you to use Tony. He's a great agent."

Interesting, isn't it? Now are you a believer?

"A digital relationship is one hundred times more powerful than a real-life relationship in the same period of time…"

By the way, scenario two with Jennifer actually happened, and it wasn't just a cute little house Jennifer bought—she and her husband bought a $3.2 million property. John, who introduced me to her at Starbucks, was her lender. John's golfing buddy was Jennifer's husband David. Of course I added David as a friend on Facebook as well. Scenarios like this have happened over and over again to me, as well as hundreds of agents whom I coach. As I started to understand the power of these digital relationships a few years ago, I asked myself while looking at my Facebook profile picture, "Who is this guy? Who is he to me? Better yet, who is he to David and Jennifer? How is this working?" You'll see me ask questions a lot in this book. I always ask myself questions. I want to see if I can increase the effectiveness of any strategy or technique. How do I make it work even more? I just keep going deeper and deeper to see what works and what doesn't. This way, not only do I benefit, but I can also help and teach others the correct ways to execute it so they benefit from it as well, which is my passion. When I asked myself, "Who is this guy?"

I realized he is my digital twin. The average human can really only know a few hundred people in his or her life. Hence how many show up to a funeral. But our digital twins have no limit to how many they can know. Why would we ever penalize our digital identity to only know the same few hundred people our own real selves can know? So who was he to me? He was my digital twin. My digital identity can be whoever I want him to be. That means he's actually the "good twin."

NOTES

CHAPTER 5

good twin | evil twin

Good twin? Think about that for a second. My digital twin doesn't get into arguments online, doesn't get in to one-sided debates, doesn't take sides religiously or politically. My digital twin is never politically incorrect. He doesn't use offensive language. See, when my digital twin goes to Las Vegas, the digital twin—you know, the good twin, just to make sure we're clear on which one we are talking about here—when he goes to Las Vegas, he just "checks in" his location to the Wynn Resort in Las Vegas, Nevada:

Tony Giordano is at **Wynn Resort, Las Vegas**
Now everybody starts commenting:

> "Oh, have fun, Tony. Put one on red 23 for me. Enjoy!"
> "Good luck, Tony!"
> "Love the Wynn. Have fun, Tony."
> "We'll be there next weekend. Can't wait. Good luck to you."
> "Enjoy the weather!"

Harmless, right? My "good twin" is in Vegas and "checked in" on Facebook. No biggie. See, the real Tony could be considered the "evil twin," if you will. I'm the one checking into the nightclub below the Wynn Resort later that night. Not that there is anything wrong with going to a nightclub. What we might be doing inside the nightclub could be dubious and/or debateable, but we don't have to get into that right now. ☺ To better understand this good twin–evil twin concept, as the evil twin, when I'm in the same room or place with my close friends and family, I might express myself in a way that my dear mother or Sunday school teacher would not appreciate.

When I'm golfing with my father and just one on one with him, I might share my extremely strong, and very angry, opinion of a certain politician running for office, but do you think my good twin online gets to?

No, he does not. That's the no-zone for the good twin. Good twin doesn't get to take sides. My good twin is everybody's friend. My good twin does not get in to political rants or religious debates. In my first edition of the book *the social agent*, I said:

> "[A] business person does not get the luxury of using social media like our friends and family do."

If you want business from it, that is. Am I telling you that you can't express yourself however you want to online? Nope. Go for it. I don't care what you do. Freedom of self-expression. I'm only telling you what gets the highest ROI building your business, and that is staying neutral. So once I started realizing this human side to social media networking, I figured out what the key was. Moving forward, I want you to all start thinking that the next time you go to post anything on your friend page of Facebook—or any social platform, actually—I want you to write it all out, and before you click the "Share" button, close your eyes and pretend that your total following or friend count is in a room with you.

EXERCISE

Think of something you want to post about right now. Maybe even write it out in your post section. Something about work, or maybe an opinion you have, anything. Now, before you click "Share," whether you have thirty friends or three thousand friends—I want you to actually close your eyes right now and picture all of them in a room with you. If you have three thousand friends, I want you to picture a massive, circular auditorium with a sea of people 360 degrees around you. You are standing onstage right in the middle of all of them. The front rows are filled with your closest friends and family, and as you look out into the distance of this large room or auditorium, your eyes start to lose focus of the individual faces and now just start to see the hundreds, if not thousands, of people who represent your following or friends online. This is very important. I want you to really put yourself there, and I want you to picture yourself standing in front of them in real time, in real life. Now, I want you to open your eyes and read word for word what you were about to post just now to them. Moving forward from now on, watch how quickly you start to change your language, if you simply think before you post and pretend you are standing in front of all of them in real time. You might be saying now, "Well, Tony, if I was in a room with all those people who are friends of mine on Facebook, I wouldn't be so boring." Yet, are we boring online?

> "New listing, four-bedroom, two-bath, Santa Monica, active, open house this Saturday between 12:00 p.m. and 4:00 p.m. Call me for details or a private showing. Entertainer's delight. Motivated seller. #NumberOne-RealEstateAgentInSantaMonicaSellingHomes"

No, see, if I was in a room with all these people online or in person, standing in front of the house, and I was talking about my new listing, I would have been in sales mode. Standing in front of the home with people, I would have said,

> "What did I tell you: think the curb appeal is beautiful? Wait till I show you the pool and outdoor kitchen you've been begging me to find you the last two months. I think this is the one; welcome home!"

But unfortunately, online, you said what 99 percent of all your competitors say about their listings in one boring way or another:

> "New listing, four-bedroom, two-bath Beverly Hills pool home, open house this Sunday between 12:00 p.m. and 4:00 p.m. Call me for details or a private showing. Entertainer's delight."

Stop turning into a robot as soon as you go online. Be the natural salesperson you are. This isn't fake. These friends of yours online are not robots. They are human beings. We haven't changed as human beings; we're just online now, that's all. It is the modern-day way we communicate, and it is equal to being in the same room with them. "Well, Tony, if I was in a room with them, I wouldn't say something so politically incorrect." Why? Because there may be someone in the audience in that auditorium who is hurt or offended by what you said, right? Then don't post it online either. "Well, Tony, if I was in a room with them, I wouldn't drop an F bomb." Then don't online. See, start pretending they're in a room with you, and watch what happens with the manner of engagement you get back online. The more you engage people, and the more you add people, the more it continues to work more and more. Growth is everything; you've got to keep adding, and you've got to keep posting. So here's the best way to think about it.

ILLUSTRATION

If you had the opportunity to be the featured guest sponsor at a business-networking event in your town where four hundred business owners and/or homeowners are going to be in attendance, and you got to get onstage and speak for ten minutes as the exclusive realtor sponsor, would you capture that opportunity? Do not tell me you would let that opportunity slip. No way you would. Your job as a marketer is what? To get in front of as many eyes and ears as you can and tell them what you do for a living. Of course you agree to this rare opportunity to build your business, and you start planning for it immediately: what you're going to say, what you're going to wear. A couple weeks later, the day of the event has arrived. They're getting ready to call you up onstage. Four hundred business owners in attendance are all starting to grab their seats and sit down. You're the only real estate agent there who gets to talk to the audience. The moment has arrived; they call your name.

> "Ladies and gentlemen, please welcome to the stage our featured sponsor and local real estate agent, John Smith..."

and you stumble out onto the stage with your shirt untucked, sloppy, slurring, sweaty drunk, double-fisting cocktails in your hand with cigarettes and say,

> "Wassup, my peeps? YEAH!!! I'm not ash think ashu drunk I am. Dohn'worry..."

Would you ever do that? Of course you wouldn't do that in person and on a stage in front of all these potential clients. But are you online? I hope not, because I see business "professionals" doing it. They have no idea just how many people they have lost as potential clients because of what they have shown online. So of course you wouldn't do that in person—I know that, obviously. You would come out on stage looking presentable. Now, I am not saying we always have to look as professional online as we would at a business-networking event. I am not saying we can't show ourselves in a bikini or board shorts, holding a margarita in our hand with an umbrella sticking out of the glass. People want to see us enjoying life, vacationing on the beach, playing with our children, and sharing our life and social side too. I'm talking about looking offensively drunk and completely unprofessional. You wouldn't do it in person with people you were trying to build a relationship with, so don't do it online. OK, let's get back to the illustration. You come onstage, you're looking presentable, and, knowing that our nation is divided on multiple levels, you know that this business networking event and audience sitting in front of you is divided on multiple levels, yet, you decide to open with,

"Before I begin, I just want to let everyone here know that I am a very outspoken Republican, and if you're not, I don't understand you."

Or:

"I am a very outspoken Democrat, and if you're not, I don't understand you."

Would you ever do that in person at a networking event? No, of course you wouldn't, but do you online? Your political party and religious beliefs show right up on your time line. Maybe you even get into debates on posts from other people on Facebook—"How can anybody be voting for him or her? I know they're stupid." Do we find ourselves taking sides? Liking Republican-related posts all the time, or liking Democrat-related posts all the time? You might as well just post them yourself, because you may not know this, but whenever you click and take any action on a post by liking or commenting on it, all your friends see you doing it. You're losing half your audience when you take sides online—in other words, half your pool of potential clients—just like you would have lost half your audience in real time at this business-networking event you are speaking on stage to.

Let's take this illustration even further. I walk up onstage, of course looking presentable, nonoffensive. I don't open with political or religious opinions, and, knowing I need to capture this audience's attention—just drive it home, make them laugh, share something personal about myself to make them feel that they are getting to know me, and make them all just love me so that we all start business-to-business (B2B) marketing together—I instead decide to do the opposite. I just stand there and say in a very monotone, boring voice:

> "Hi, my name is Tony Giordano. I'm a real estate agent with the Opulent Agency Inc. here in Los Angeles, California. If I could get your attention to the slide on the screen, this is a new listing of mine. Five bedrooms, two baths, Santa Monica. Motivated seller. Pool home. Open this Saturday between noon and four p.m. Send me your buyers if you know anyone, or call me for details for a showing.
>
> "Next slide, please. This is a price reduction of a house we listed thirty days ago. Now definitely a motivate seller. Open this Sunday between noon and four p.m. Call me for details. Send me your buyers.
>
> "Next slide, please. Oh, this is a four-hundred-thousand-dollar condo we just closed sale on. Market is really heating up.
>
> "Next slide, please. This is another closing that we just had today for a home that we had the pleasure of representing the sellers on for one-point-three million. Market's hot, like I said before.

"Next slide, please. Oh, these are my designations I have been certified as a specialist in. As you can see, I'm CREA, GREEN, SRS...ABC, DEF, GHI, JKL, **OMG, LOL, TTYL**

"Next slide, please. This is an award that I won for being in the top one percent of my company nationally. It was a really amazing award to receive because only a few people make the top one percent.

"Next slide, please. This is another price reduction of another listing we have on the market. Let me know if you think you know anyone who may want to see it."

What would you be doing right now if you were sitting in that audience at the business-networking event? No question you would be thinking, *Get off the stage. This is why I hate real estate agents. Me, me, me, me. Boring, boring, boring, boring, boring.* Would you ever do that in person at a networking event? No, of course not. You would have come out onstage and said:

"Hi everybody, thank you for having me today. Yes, I'm a real estate agent here in LA, but that's not what I'm passionate about. What I'm really passionate about is being a father to two amazing sons named Michael and Christopher. Actually, that reminds me of something funny that happened with my son yesterday. We were eating ice cream, and he started to make this really bad frown on his face but kept eating ice cream, and I asked him, 'What's wrong, Christopher?' He said, 'I have a really bad brain freeze.' I said, 'Then why do you keep eating more?' He said, 'Uhh, because it's ice cream?' [Audience LAUGHS]

"They were born and raised here in LA, as I was too. My whole family is from here, actually.

"But what I'd like to do now is, I don't want to take the fifteen minutes that I have been so kindly given from you today as a sponsor. I'd rather come off the stage right now and enjoy some wine and hors d'oeuvres with all of you, shake your hands and get to know one another. Also, when I come up to you, if you could please have your business card ready so that you can tell me what you do for a living. I'd like to see how I can send my clients and my database to you and help your business grow. Thanks again for letting me have this opportunity, and let's have some fun this evening."

Now what are you thinking as you sit in the audience? "Yes, this speaker I can handle; he's making it about us." That's what you would have done in person. But are we doing that online? No, we are not. Online is:

"New listing!" POST
"New listing!" POST
"Another new listing." POST
"Under contract." POST

"Another one under contract." POST
"Price reduced." POST
"Price reduced." POST
"Open..." POST
"Just closed!" POST
"Open..." POST
"Open again..." POST
"Price reduced." POST
"I love referrals!" POST

Really? You love referrals? That's awesome. Thank you so much for telling me that you love referrals, because I didn't think you liked referrals, and I had like nine referrals to give you in the last year, but I thought you didn't like them. So I gave them to someone else. But now that you've stated the obvious here, I'll start giving them to you in the future. (Blink, blink)

So many people are losing the human factor as soon as they go online. They lose all human sales ability. From this point on, start pretending that with everything you want to post and say online, you would say to an audience or with potential clients actually standing alongside you. Watch your natural language of sales kick in online now too. Then there is the whole aspect of having manners online. If we were standing in front of each other with a group of people, and I complimented you for something, wouldn't you say thank you? Yes, you would. But are you doing that online? You post something, people start commenting on your post, and you don't even take two seconds to at least click the "Like" button on their comment? They took time out of their day to comment and engage your post, and you just go about your day without acknowledging them back? You wouldn't do that in person, so don't do it online. Manners apply online as well.

IT'S ABOUT THEM, NOT YOU

Here is a very simple approach and blueprint to follow when posting content to your social media profiles. When does someone feel a need to go on a social network just to scroll around and see what everyone else is doing? We are not talking about when someone is excited to go online and share something. I'm asking, when do people, or even you reading this right now, feel a need to just go online and surf around news feeds on social networks? Yep, you guessed it:

- ☐ Bored
- ☐ Downtime, nonengaged at the moment
- ☐ Lonely
- ☐ Depressed
- ☐ At work...lol.

Well, then think about this for minute: You really think someone who is bored wants to go online and see your boring, business-related posts? What do people really want to see? Here are by far the top five greatest categories of content that will get you more positive engagement than any other categories of content. No, I don't mean babies and cats when I say "categories." I mean how is the baby and cat making you feel? What is a particular post helping you with? Or why is a certain post causing you to engage with it more than another? These are the top five categories of high engagement.

THE HIGH FIVE (H-FIVE)

H. HEARTFELT

This is by far the number-one category over any other. The amount of positive engagement that happens in this category dominates any other. In the category of heartfelt, you have various levels and feelings. Here are just a few to help you understand.

- [ ] Someone beat cancer
- [ ] Someone did not beat cancer
- [ ] An animal was saved
- [ ] Someone changed the course of another person's life for the better
- [ ] Passion (your "Big Why")
- [ ] Motivational
- [ ] Inspirational

So can babies and cats touch your heart? Sure, so they can fall in the heartfelt category. But can they also make you laugh? Yes. So we are not talking about a particular thing like a cat or baby, we are talking about categories of how the post is making you react regardless of what thing is in it. Oh and side note, if you do not know what a "Big Why" is or means, read the best-selling book *A Joy Filled Life* by Mo Anderson, who is like a mother to me. OK, after Heartfelt, that brings us to the second-highest category for the amount of positive engagement that will come from it...

F. FUNNY

There is no question people want to laugh. This category always has an extremely high percentage of engagement from your friends or following online. Although high, it doesn't come close to heartfelt. But humor is also very important to think about in your content. Funny photos, funny videos, or maybe something funny that happened to you—or you say something funny. If you are naturally funny, be funny. If you are not naturally funny, *do not* try to be funny. Lol. Google "Funny Quotes" and copy and paste a funny phrase or sentence and post it.

I. INTERESTS

This category of a *happy life* is exactly what it means: posts and content that simply show you enjoying life. Examples would be:

- ☐ Family gatherings, holidays, vacations
- ☐ Kids' sports

- ☐ Proud dad or mom moments (not overboard, please)
- ☐ Time with friends
- ☐ Travel
- ☐ Sunbathing on a tropical beach
- ☐ Surfing with your kids

V. VALUE

Our natural human nature is to help one another. At least the good humans want to help each other, that is. We all love giving and receiving value. When we give each other value, it deepens relationships. We see this when we go online and ask for help or assistance. Example, you go online and ask a question like, "Does anyone know where I can find a good painter?" All of a sudden, everyone and their grandma comes chiming in for the first time in two years and leaves a comment on your post to help you. This is when you may think to yourself, *Wow, people really do see my posts...well, wait—that means they just never comment on them?* Hmm. Maybe that is because you are not posting along the lines of the High Five categories? Trust me, people see your posts. You want to challenge me on this? Challenge accepted. If you really want to see how many of your friends or following actually see your posts, go online right now and say something like, "So what do you all think about the president?" You already know I won this challenge now. Trust me when I say, most of your friends see your posts. By the way, *do not* ask that question. Lol.

E. EDUCATIONAL

We all love to learn and build wisdom in life. Knowledge is power. People love being educated; however, there are ways to educate and ways *not* to educate.

- ☐ Be clever. The cleverer we are in educating our friends and following, the better received it will be.
- ☐ Don't be boring. We have already talked about this. There are plenty of ways to educate people in a nonboring way. Be the fun teacher you remember from school, not the teacher you never paid attention to.
- ☐ Short and sweet. The faster they are able to read or watch it and learn something, the more valuable you are, and the more engagement you will get.

Sample Educational Post:

RIGHT WAY: "Saint County Medical Center to expand ER to a Level 1 Trauma Center for 300 million."

WRONG WAY: "Today I was reading an article that said that our local Saint County Medical Center was going to be expanding their Emergency Room to a Level 1 Trauma Center for 300 million dollars!!!??? For those who don't know what a level-one trauma center is, it is the highest level emergency room there can be. It takes the gunshot victims, stab wounds, missing limbs, helicopter fly-ins. The article went on to say that it was going to cost 300 million dollars? I can't help but ask myself, well, who is paying for that? Is the hospital paying for that, or are we, the local taxpayers, paying for it? Because I swear, if I have to pay for another thing..."

...and by this point, you're thinking to yourself, *Why am I still reading this?* Remember, short and sweet. They were able to read it, learn something, and move on with their day.

Another Example:

RIGHT WAY: "Local housing market up 5.8 percent from this time last year. More info @ www.theopulentagency.com."

WRONG WAY: "The real estate housing market is up 5.8 percent from this time last year. Last year at this time, the market had seen a 4.7 percent increase since the same time the year before that. I, and many of my fellow agents thought there was no way it would have another strong year, but sure enough, we've seen another 5 percent–plus increase. Now this is due to the ever-growing issue of low inventory and the high demand of buyers trying to take advantage of buying a home with record-breaking low interest rates along with a strong luxury real estate market being fueled by foreign money pouring in to America's housing market and stable economy..." Blah, blah, blah. *Get out of my news feed!*

The High Five (H-FIVE) categories of content are really what people want to see, starting at the most preferred category of heartfelt and dropping in the level of "positive relationship building" engagement as you go down each category. However, all the H-FIVE are very important to do when posting content to the world. Everything else is **far** below in interest to people. Boring business, bragging, one-sided rants or opinions, politically incorrect posts, hate, racism, and overall offensive content... nothing positive will come out of any of these low-level, narrow-minded posts.

NOTES

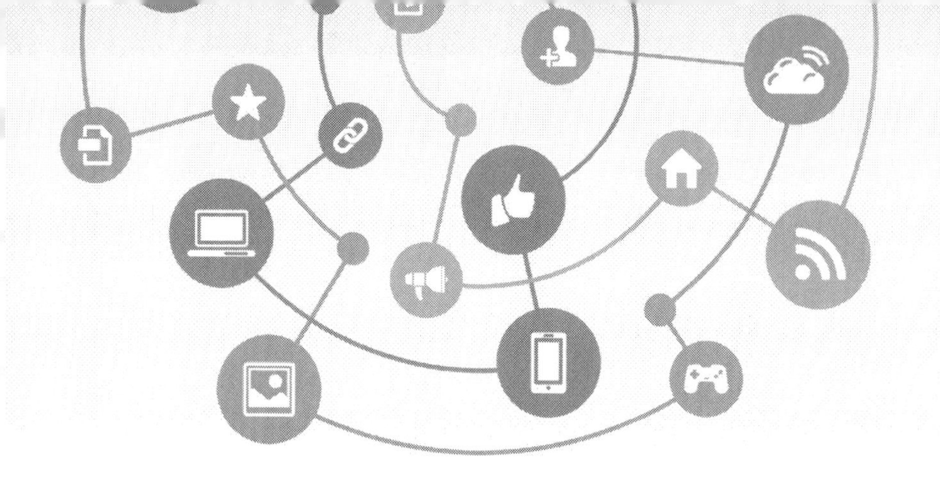

CHAPTER 6

the "visual" approach

www.instagram.com/tony_giordano

Personally, I consider Instagram the "visual" network. However, it started as the "photo" network. Yes there are Pinterest, Snapchat, and others out there. Even Facebook is considered a visual network. Instagram has mastered it, though. This network came on the scene and exploded very quickly because it was simple, and everyone loves photos online. Especially selfies.

Don't do that, please. ☺

Instagram's rise got Mark Zuckerberg's curiosity pretty quickly, but when Instagram hit fifty million users, now it had Mark's attention. Around this time it became pretty common knowledge that Facebook was purchasing Instagram for a billion dollars. Maybe some of you heard the joke back then:

> "I don't know why Mark Zuckerberg bought Instagram for a billion dollars? He could have just downloaded the app for free." ☺

Personally, I thought the acquisition was genius on Mark's part. Fitting, right—because we know he is a genius at this point. I believe he saw Instagram as the photo giant, and as Google owns YouTube (meaning Google owns video), why wouldn't Facebook want to own photo? It makes perfect sense to me.

THE INSTAGRAM APPROACH

This network is a marketing beast in every aspect. Here is the thing, though: since Instagram is no longer only about photos; it has continued to innovate and release more features, taking it into the video and visual story space. Its niche is self-expression visually, not written text. The photo, video, story is what needs to capture the user's attention. Users swipe the news feed on Instagram with their fingers faster than on any other network. We are swiping and scrolling down until something captures our eye, and only then do we stop to look at it. We are not swiping slowly to read the description of the photo that someone wrote. Why? Well, what are users looking for when they log into Instagram? That's right, photos and videos. That is what we are in the mood for at that moment—and not just any photos and videos; we want captivating photos and videos. We will discuss video marketing in much more depth in Chapter 10.

So what questions should you ask yourself before becoming an active user on Instagram?

> "Do I love photography? Do I enjoy it? Do I have an eye for it? Do I love video? Do I love expressing myself with video?"

This will help you determine if you should spend time on it. Here is a way to know whether you belong on this network. Compare the next two examples.

Let's say you and another person are taking the same photo of a gorgeous sunset. You take your phone out of your pocket, raise it up, and...snap! All done; you post it on Instagram to your few hundred followers and say,

> "Enjoying a gorgeous sunset in Malibu."

Now your friend goes to take the same photo while standing in the same spot you did. He grabs his phone out of his pocket, and immediately, as a creature of habit, you see him wipe the lens of his phone off with his T-shirt to prevent any blurring or fingerprint smudges. He now raises the phone up and looks at the image, only to realize the angle is horrible. He starts to walk a little to the left, trying to find that perfect angle where he can hide the power lines you didn't notice. Finally he gets a good spot where he can hide the power lines with a palm tree. Now you see your friend move just a tad to the right so the sun is shining through the palm tree, creating amazing reflections and lines of rays in the image. Then, right before he takes the shot, he sees in his peripheral vision a seagull flying closer, so he waits just two extra seconds and snaps the shot with the bird gliding through. Shot complete. At this point, your friend opens his Instagram app, and you notice he is going through all these different filters on the photo and editing the photo to capture its best features and colors. Finally, after another couple of minutes go by, he is ready to post it. He first tags the location of the photo as the "City of Malibu." Second, he posts it on Instagram to his two hundred followers and says:

"Enjoying a gorgeous #Sunset in #Malibu #California."

As a few minutes go by, you both start getting likes and comments on your photos from your followers. Within thirty minutes, you have thirteen likes and no comments, and your friend has sixty-seven likes and eleven comments. Why such a big difference?

Well, your photo had those power lines in it, didn't show all the palm trees, your lens was a little smudged, and your finger was just a little in the way in the corner of the photo. Long story short, your friend belongs on Instagram; you don't.

Shall we go further down the rabbit hole?

In addition to this, your friend's post that he wrote, although similar to most people's, was light-years more effectively thought out. First he tagged the location of where he was standing, which put him in a photo album of everyone who has ever taken a photo there. Now total strangers who aren't among his two hundred followers are seeing it also. Another thing he did differently was that he used hashtags. This technique also placed him in a photo album news feed of all the other hundreds of people who are posting photos with the hashtags #sunset, #malibu, and #california. This resulted in your friend not only getting more likes and comments, but he also got some new followers from the post as well. Any reason I should explain the boring algorithms that make this possible? No, there is no reason I should bore you with this. You're welcome! Just do it; you don't need to know how it works. You only need to know how to get the results.

What would be an example of those techniques in a real estate or business-related post?

Now your followers will be like, "Oh wow, what a cool angle of that house with Tony's sign over the pool." So they stopped and now—"I wonder if this is one of his new listings?" And now they see right below the photo: "New listing in #Santa Monica (blah, blah, blah) #LosAngeles #BeverlyHills #Brentwood." Now they could see what I wrote there. But otherwise they swiped and flew right by it.

INSTAGRAM—SOCIAL VERSUS BUSINESS

In my personal opinion, if you are in sales or own a business, you should have a minimum of two Instagram accounts. Just as Twitter does, Instagram makes it very easy to hop or switch between multiple accounts that you have so you don't have to log out of Instagram and relog into your other account. You can just bounce back and forth and use it as the account you're in at that moment. This makes it easy for me to see it as one of my companies—take, for instance, @TheOpulentAgency—or if I want, I just switch it to my personal account, @Tony_Giordano.

My account @Tony_Giordano is very close to my Facebook friend page. It's mostly social and every now and then business. Maybe a photo of my listing, maybe a cool picture of my "For Sale" signs, maybe me speaking onstage, but otherwise, for the most part, it will be my personal life through my lens. Travel, family, friends, moti- vational, inspirational, heartfelt, funny...very similar to Facebook and following the HIGH FIVE (H-FIVE) of content; however, because of the variety of demographics and global reach, both Instagram and Facebook serve their own unique purpose.

Here is an example of what a personal Instagram can achieve or be used for and the power of Instagram today versus Facebook yesterday. My girlfriend and I were in Napa Valley for a conference I was speaking at. We decided to make a weekend of it and went wine tasting, of course, because obviously it would be dumb not to go wine tasting if you're in #NapaValley speaking, right? We decided to go to the winery of my girlfriend's favorite wine, Cake Bread Cellars. While on the tour, we took a photo of us drinking wine, and we uploaded the photo on Facebook, checked in on the location on Facebook at Cake Bread Cellars, and posted it.

After Facebook, we got on Instagram and did the same thing. We did not feed it in to Facebook from Instagram, as fewer people see it when you feed posts in from somewhere else. You want to try and always post inside each network directly. We posted the same photo, checked in to the winery location on Instagram as well, mentioned @cakebreadcellars Instagram account, and also threw a couple

#'s hashtags (for our older ones the pound sign, or for our really older ones, the tic-tac-toe game) on a couple of the words in our post. My girlfriend thought of something super clever to say in this photo of the two of us "cheersing":

> **@londonhowe**
> "Having our cake and drinking it too w/ @tony_giordano"—@CakeBreadCellars #CakeBreadCellars #CakeBreadWine

Brilliant, right? Yeah, that's my girlfriend London, for you.

About ten minutes after the post, we're on the wine tour with six other couples, and a manager comes over to us. (Obviously he recognizes my bald head from the Instagram post.)

> MANAGER: "Tony? London?"
> ME: "Yeah?"
> MANAGER: "Thank you so much for checking in online. Come and see me afterward; I have a gift for you."

As he walked away, another couple on the tour with us looked at us with jealous eyes.

> COUPLE: "What the heck?"
> ME: "Well, we checked in, and I think they are just appreciating us for it, so he wants to give us a free bottle of wine."
> COUPLE: "Well, we checked in too."

ME: "What network did you check in on? Because we did Facebook and Instagram."

COUPLE: "Well, we just did Facebook. I didn't even know you could check in on Instagram."

ME: "Yes, you can check in on almost every network out there. The reason he probably came up to us and gave us the bottle of wine was because a few years ago, when you did that on Facebook at a restaurant, what did they do? They gave you a free appetizer, right? Remember that? Check in on Facebook, we'll give you a free round of drinks. That was because they were building their Facebook presence still. However, now it's built. They don't need to give away anything for Facebook anymore. They have a massive audience on Facebook now; they've got it down. It works; it makes them money. People check in all the time to their restaurant on Facebook. Their audience is there; they love it. Now they're building their Instagram accounts, and we helped build it right then and there when we checked in during this wine tour. So now they're simply doing on Instagram what they did on Facebook a few years ago."

NOTE: It was about a $100 bottle of wine he gave us, and when I saw it in the cabinet, I was like, "Yeah! I love Instagram."

That's one social aspect to Instagram. Here's another social aspect of Instagram and how it is being used today. While we were on vacation in Tulum, Mexico, the entire Caribbean side of Quintana Roo was going through one of the worst natural die-offs of seaweed in the ocean in about twenty years. All the beaches along the Caribbean had this high pile of black seaweed that you had to walk over to get to the water that then was just brown and murky as well. Every twenty years or so, I guess it happens, and it's just a massive die-off of seaweed, and it ruins all the beaches that summer. Well, it was ruining people's vacations, too, and when we got there, we couldn't believe how bad it was—we'd had no clue it was even happening. First time we ever went to Tulum, and that ruined it. For a couple of days, we were looking for other places to go so that we could just pack up and drive somewhere else down the coastline for the remaining seven days and hope to find white sand beaches and gorgeous turquoise water. A friend who was with us started looking on Google Maps, and we found a place called Punta Allen, about two hours south from Tulum. Our friend started looking at Google Images of Punta Allen, and she showed us dozens of gorgeous pictures of this place—snorkeling, diving, white sand beaches, turquoise water—just gorgeous photos on Google Images.

OUR FRIEND, DIANE: "We've got to go."
ME: "Diane? How old do you think Google Images are?"
DIANE: "What do you mean?"
ME: "What images do you think are in Google when you Google something? They're the best, the best of the best for the last five years. Right?"
DIANE: "Oh yes, I guess?"

I grabbed my phone and opened up Instagram, went to the search bar of Instagram, and searched the hashtag #PuntaAllen, and it pulled up dozens and dozens of photos of Punta Allen by people who lived there, tourists, and so on. When do you think those photos were taken? That's right, that day. There were dozens of photos that day actually, and the day before, and the day before that, and so on. And what do you think we could see all over the beach in the images? The same thing: the black, murky water, with dead seaweed piling up on the entire strand of beach. Just saved us a two-hour drive to Punta Allen. If I had thought of using Instagram like that before flying to Cancun, it would have saved us even more time and money. I use Instagram and look at photos of people visiting anywhere I'm going now, days or even weeks in advance. Eventually we found photos of a place on the other side of Cancun, with gorgeous, clear water and no seaweed, so we hopped in the Jeep, canceled the rest of our stay in Tulum, drove two and a half hours to the other side, and stayed there for the remaining days and had an amazing vacation. We fell in love with the island as well. (Sorry, the location is top secret.)

That's another example of the power of what's happening online today and using these social networks in so many different ways. People are starting to search for photos and videos of things that are happening on that day of places they are traveling to, or even places they are moving to. Hmm? Would you say it's important, then, that any time you're posting any photos, especially anything related to real estate, you should have hashtags on your description of the cities in which you sell real estate?

> #LosAngeles; #BeverlyHills; #Brentwood; #Hollywood; #SantaMonica; #Malibu; #ManhattanBeach; #HermosaBeach...

...because people are going to be searching for photos of your areas on Instagram, and it's becoming more and more of a trend. Whose brand do you want them to see? Yours. They're going to see your listings, right? They're going to see your brand, right? If they're moving to your area, they will search for photos of your area, and as it continues gaining steam and it becomes more and more something that people do, then you must act accordingly.

INSTAGRAM—BUSINESS VERSUS SOCIAL

In addition to my social page, I have to have my real estate and/or business Instagram page. My producing real estate team, the Opulent Agency, should have its own as well. But now, instead of social, it's going to be mostly what? It's going to be mostly real estate–related visual posts, like photos and videos. Examples of posts include, but are not limited to, a video for our new listings or a picture of the ocean view from the balcony of a new listing we are having an open house on. Maybe it's a before-and-after series of photos from staging the property that we posted. Our brand, "For Sale" signs, cities in which we sell real estate, or simply clever things that we come up with every now and then just to get content out there to brand ourselves in our communities. If we are posting about our brand or listings, then we're going to #hashtag all the surrounding cities of Los Angeles on the listing, not just the city the listing is in.

Whether it is a photo, or a video that you are posting, the more you learn and get in the habit of #hashtagging, the more you increase your overall following, and the more effective it becomes. I have heard my coaching clients tell me time and time again how they have moved a listing because they are #hashtagging better, gained a buyer because they are #hashtagging better, gained a seller because they are #hashtagging better, and so on.

Let's not forget who owns Instagram: Mr. Zuckerberg, of course. This means, as the platform continues to be built, modified, and updated, it will increasingly have more uses as time goes on and social and digital communication continues to evolve. An example of this would be running marketing campaigns and sponsored ads—at a cost, of course—on the platform. There is no reason to get into this right now; as you will see in chapter 11, we will discuss the "targeting" approach of various platforms, including Instagram. We will also discuss the power of video marketing in chapter 10 which will include Instagram once again, along with YouTube.

THE POWER OF INSTAGRAM PRESENCE

I recall, not that long ago, speaking at an event where the topic was just Instagram. It was a three-hour presentation on advanced Instagram strategy. When I left the stage, a gentleman came up to me and said that he was so happy that he came to the event because he had known the power of social media and online presence; however, he had not figured out how to truly apply it in his business. We spoke for a good fifteen minutes or so, and although I had given him a hundred techniques to go back home and do that day, he would end up only implementing about 20 percent of what he learned that day and completely changing his way of life. Per his request in wanting to stay anonymous so his competition doesn't know how he did it and continues to do it, I have changed the city location and his name. Let's name him Jack for the sake of his example.

After the event, he flew home to Chicago and immediately started to implement a few of the strategies he learned.

The next morning he was walking in the city on his way to his office, and he went to a new high-rise building that was not only a hotel, it was also residential units that had started selling about a year prior. Now something you also need to understand is that this agent was a rookie. He had been a licensed agent for barely nine months and only had a couple closings under his belt. It was an absolutely gorgeous day in Chicago this particular morning. As he approached the tower, he noticed the sun was just behind the very top of the tower with the rays of light shining off the corner of the building and a stunning blue sky in the backdrop. Hundreds of people were walking each way in the intersection and sidewalks, heading to work. Standing in front of the tower was a doorman, very well dressed, guiding guests who were pulling up in front in the valet and walking them up the red carpet through the beautiful glass lobby doors. The agent grabbed his phone and looked for the perfect spot to snap a photo of the building. As he moved to different spots across the street, trying to get the entire building in the shot, he finally found the perfect angle. As people walked all around him, he knelt way down, resting his knee on the ground, aimed up toward the sun, slightly moved his phone lens to the left to get the majestic rays of light shining off the top of the tower, and snapped the image. At this point Jack had already invested about ten minutes in his day getting this image just right. Sound familiar? Who belongs on Instagram? ☺

However, he was not even kind of done with his investment of time yet. At this point he opened his Instagram app on his phone, started to look through the dozen or so different images he had shot, and found the one he felt had the best angle that captured his own eye and liking. As he looked at the image, he noticed that it might look a little better if he cropped out another building on the right side of it, so he did. He then went into the filters and found one that brought out the sun and sky at a higher contrast and really made the photo pop more. After editing the image, he wrote a description for it:

> "Every morning when I walk by this building, I am in awe of its beauty. Not only an elite hotel, but some of the most luxurious apartments and penthouses in #Chicago. I love showing these residences any chance I get, so if you have an interest in a private showing, please contact me for details. #DowntownChicago #ChicagoLand #ChicagoRealEstate #LuxuryRealEstate #WindyCity"

Let me give you some more details about what would add to the powerful outcome that this post ended up achieving. Before he posted it, he also tagged and "@" mentioned the building's own Instagram account and "checked in" to its location in his post. Once Jack had finished all that, he clicked the "Share" tab. For about an hour, he received dozens of likes and comments from people complimenting him on the great photo and/or sharing their thoughts about the location. One of these comments would change everything, though. It would be a comment from the hotel's Instagram account, from the residential management office.

> MANAGEMENT: "Thank you for sharing such a beautiful picture of our building. We love showing our residences too. Will you please contact us at the office? We would like to speak with you."
> JACK: "Of course, and look forward to meeting you."

This agent at first thought he was in trouble when they asked him to call them. Was he not supposed to take a photo of the building? Should he not have said he was available to show it? These were actual thoughts he told me were going through his mind at that moment. When he contacted the management office, they asked him if he was a top agent and team in the Chicago area. After I coached him through answering their questions, they then relayed the following: "We have had these units listed for sale for eleven months and have been begging our current listing brokerage for this kind of marketing for a year now, and they still have yet to do so or even show us they know how to execute it. We have no intentions of renewing our agreement with them and would like to meet with you and your team to discuss the potential opportunity to market our units as our listing agent."

After a lot more coaching with him, and multiple discussions with them, he ended up getting the listing. Very long story short, within one year he had sold and/or leased out 70 percent of the tower. This particular listing would catapult his career and became the driving machine that brought him even more opportunities, both locally and globally. All from doing what? One morning he decided to take a picture of a building and post it. Was it the way he posted it, though, that led to the success? Most certainly. There is an art to everything, and there is truly an art to online presence and social media marketing.

THE DIFFERENCES

The majority of these large networks have many similarities, and although I could write a book this size on each one of the PERFECT 10, it is not needed. Why? Simple. When we overthink these social media networks, we lose the effectiveness. Why do we make sales and building relationships so difficult? I said it earlier: "Sales is a _________ game!" *Numbers.* Don't overthink these networks. Don't overcomplicate them.

> "The number-one rule of lead generation is go where the people are."
> — #TonyG

If you understand this, then it is easy to understand each network, what its niche is, and what value it has to you and your brand. Just like Instagram is the "visual" network, I can also build my brand visually and draw traffic to my business using Pinterest and Snapchat. There will be some slight differences in the techniques, but not much.

"SNAP IT"

Snapchat came on the scene and very quickly became a force to be reckoned with. Mainly it was its niche, as we have been talking about. If you have a great niche, you can dominate very fast. That is why I have them in my PERFECT 10 list. Snapchat's niche was short-duration video. In other words, it was self-expression in a few seconds through a video that, once you shared it to your own selective audience, would disappear shortly after, as if it never happened. At the beginning of this book, though, we discussed that Snapchat is losing its niche to Instagram. If it is not careful, we could most likely see them get acquired by a larger company. As I said before, though, you need to have a Snapchat account, become familiar with it, and make sure people can find you on it. Many of the techniques and the approaches that you have already learned so far in this book, along with what you learn in the upcoming chapters, you can do on Snapchat as well. We shall see what their fate ends up being.

"PIN IT"

Pinterest is the "interest" network, or also known as "Fantasy Football" for women. ☺ Now, if you are a woman who loves Fantasy Football as well, I meant no disrespect. Lol. Since the beginning of Pinterest, its dominant user demographic has been female. Although millions of males have Pinterest accounts, the majority of all the activity inside Pinterest—meaning the pinning, messaging, activity, and shopping—is still predominantly female. It is not that hard to believe. Think about what it is: retail, shopping, design, recipes, fashion, "best of" reviews…so many more aspects to Pinterest I could mention. Those are just aspects of life that naturally most women are more drawn to than most men. So if you're single, and like women, you're welcome. I just told you where you should be spending most of your time. ☺

As a trainer and coach, I have well over ten hours of curriculum on Pinterest techniques and strategy. I break them down to Pinterest 1.0, 2.0, and Pinterest Advanced Workshops. I've seen many agents I coach capture business and build their brands within Pinterest. They have been very successful growing their overall influence and following. These agents are very active in the network, though. I think Pinterest is an absolute marketing beast, which is why I teach it and help many to learn how to use it, but it's just not my thing. I don't actively Pinterest every day, all day. But I do know the importance of having a Pinterest presence, so I will just have someone on my team keep my account active for me so I don't have to myself, since it's just not my thing. You know, when I shop and buy shoes, I just buy the shoes. I don't need to pin the photo of my new shoes, so they go to my Pinterest wallboard, so my bros see the shoes and are like, "Dude, look at Tony's new shoes. Man, one day I want those shoes…" so then they "pin" the shoes, too, as "one day" dream shoes to buy, and we're all just buying and dreaming about shoes together. ☺

So if Pinterest is not my thing, then why do I have one? Why do I have a dynamic and very active profile that draws traffic to my brand and websites, if it's not my thing? SEO, for one. But mostly it is for this reason: just because it's not my thing doesn't mean it's not someone else's thing. There are millions upon millions of people on Pinterest worldwide, which means there are thousands upon thousands of people in my local area who are on it every day, every hour, on the hour. How could this prove to be beneficial to you or your brand? Here is just one very simple example of how I have personally benefited from it with a woman I got as a client from having Pinterest presence. I love to track where my clients come from, so when I interviewed her, here is what I found out.

A woman was referred to me by a friend of hers because she was going to be selling her home and buying another soon. She was also referred to another agent from a different friend of hers who was also trying to help her. A couple days had gone by, and she hadn't called me or the other agent yet. She was not in a hurry and would start doing her research on us when she was ready. One day that same week, she was in Pinterest, like she is every hour on the hour, just scrolling through the feed of posts from recipes, high heels, dresses, travel…and then she happens to see a picture of a backyard with a stunning swimming pool. Well, that just happened to be the reason she was selling her home in the first place—because she wanted a bigger yard with a swimming pool. When she saw that photo, it reminded her: "Oh, I still need to call those two real estate agents and start to figure out which one I am going to hire. I wonder if they have Pinterest?"

SEARCH: Tony Giordano
"Oh yes, real estate agent; this has to be him."
CLICK: Follow (Starts to look at my profile)

"Oh wow! I like his style. I've read that book too. Look at these houses he has on his profile! I wonder if some of these are his listings. Wow, that's a gorgeous one. Definitely couldn't afford that, but I'm going to pin it and add it to my Pinterest profile in my 'Dream Homes' album."

After pinning it, she also opened the photo to see what website the picture came from. All photos you see on Pinterest are tied to a website. For example, you see this dress you can't live without, and when you open that photo on Pinterest, you click the link, and all of a sudden you are on that retail brand's website with a big "Buy" button under that dress.

So when she opened my photo, what website did she end up on? My website. Why or how? Because Mopro (website company) makes all the photos of our listings "pinnable." I can't say it enough. They are geniuses. Let's go further down the Pinterest rabbit hole, shall we?

"Pinnable" Website Photo

"Pinned" Pinterest Photo

After she pinned the photo of my listing, her 2,350 followers on Pinterest saw that she pinned my photo because everything is tracked. As soon as you take an action, your "following" sees it. Now, all her friends saw this action, and maybe a few of them pinned the same photo—or better yet, ended up on my site. Long story short, she felt connected with me pretty quickly, sent me a message on Pinterest. I called her, and I ended up selling her home and helping her buy a new one. Just because Pinterest is not my thing, per se, does not mean it's not someone else's thing. My job is not to assume people on Pinterest are not leads. My job is to be findable and have presence within any network that has millions upon millions of people and say to them all, "I'm here. I'm an agent. If you'd like to contact me here, I am available to you." That's our job as sales professionals, to market ourselves. Just like it's my job to market my client's listing as soon as I get it. That means putting their homes in front of as many eyes and ears as I can and telling them it is for sale—exactly the same thing we need to do when marketing ourselves. A potential customer researching us will easily decide not to call us and come to this realization. "Why on earth would I ever trust this person to market my home, when I can easily see online he or she doesn't even know how to market him- or herself?" We are marketers long before we are sales-people.

NOTES

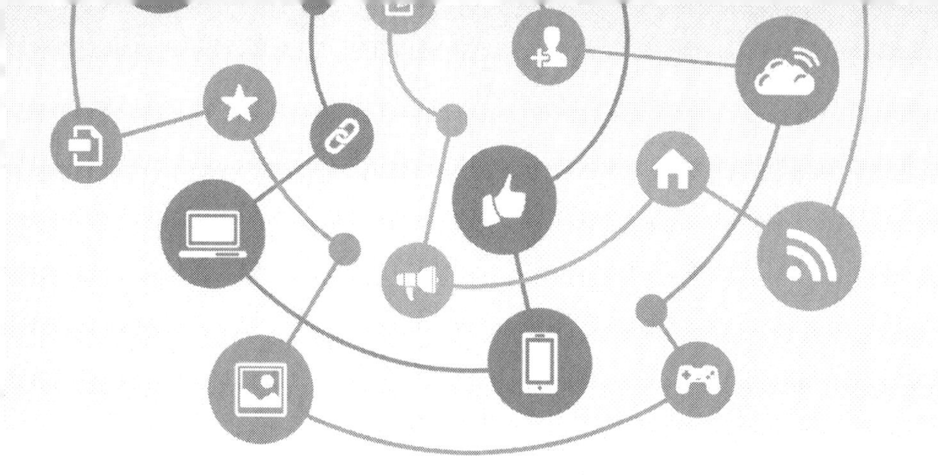

CHAPTER 7

the "professional" approach

www.linkedin.com/in/thesocialagent

LinkedIn is simply the modern day résumé. It is a professional network of connections and branding. It took LinkedIn a decade to reach two hundred million people, and now it has two people joining every second. When is the last time you heard a Monster.com commercial? No, not the energy drink, the job-recruiting website. Not often anymore. That is because in recent years, LinkedIn has risen as the number-one network, for professionals, job seekers, and job recruiters (headhunters) in the world. Linkedin is also owned by, some guy you may have heard of before, named Mr. Bill Gates. In *the social agent*, first edition, I stated that LinkedIn has the highest average income per user of any "social network." That is still the case. Recently the network lowered the age limit to thirteen years old. That's right. Thirteen! When I say that onstage to an audience, I usually hear a big "Huh?" travel across the assembly hall. Most wonder why LinkedIn would lower the age threshold to thirteen. I am here to tell you why. You see, nothing has changed from twenty years ago. When I was thirteen and getting ready to start high school and wanted a job as a part-time lifeguard, what did I need to give the employer when I went in for an interview? You guessed it—a résumé, right? It makes perfect sense that a thirteen-year-old would have a résumé online, especially if he or she is seeking a job soon. We have all heard of young inventors and innovators as well.

LinkedIn isn't just for individual professionals or companies. Universities are not only on LinkedIn, but some of them research LinkedIn to scout talented teens for scholarships. So now I only have one question to ask you. Are you proud of your online résumé? Do you draw traffic to it? Is it complete? What would have happened years ago if you walked in to a job interview and handed the employer a résumé half complete, with a coffee mug stain on one of the corners of your 8x11 "masterpiece"? Let's just say you probably wouldn't have made it to the second interview. Now of course that wasn't the case for us back then, right? What did we do? We were proud of our résumés. Maybe we had it all completed on one page, making it easy for potential employers to review it. Maybe we used a thicker stock paper to rise above the competition. Maybe we even laminated it. We did whatever we could do to that 8½x11 piece of paper to stand out from the other applicants.

Now, I know some of you reading this, are probably saying, "Well, I already have my career established. Why do I need a résumé?" Fair enough, but if people are what drive your income, and you are in sales, then your career is only as strong as your last sale. Last client. Last patient. Last contact. Your employer doesn't necessarily need to see your modern-day résumé, but your clients do. See, in sales, it is a contact sport, and we interview for a job every day. Oh, and if you don't think your potential clients are looking at you online before they call you, you are mistaken. You would be surprised how many consumers Google us and view us on LinkedIn before making the call. You know it is true, because you Google everyone too. Ever notice how LinkedIn is often on the first page of Google results when you're searching a professional's name? After people click on your profile, LinkedIn then notifies you that someone has viewed your profile, right? We, of course, click to see who has viewed our profile, but LinkedIn only teases us with two or three people, and if you want to see the entire list, you have to upgrade to a premium account and pay for LinkedIn. It is only becoming more and more common for us to be Googled and researched as humans continue to gain access to info so quickly. It is at our fingertips, even when we are on the go. What should your résumé look like? Well, just like that 8½x11 piece of paper back in the day or the one you attach to e-mails or sales presentations today, your LinkedIn profile should crush it. Some of you may have your LinkedIn built out already to a degree, and I am sure I can add to it.

TIP #1: COMPLETE YOUR ONLINE RÉSUMÉ

First and foremost, **before you even start** driving traffic to your profile or building relationships, you must update and complete your profile. Be very detailed and give it everything. Just like years ago, or even your résumé on paper today, you have your contact info, phone, e-mail, references, education, all work experience. You have an objective, or your "headline" of what you do. If you are seeking a job, of course you want your profile to show that. If you are seeking new clients, then you want your headline to be a quick blurb on why they should contact you. If you want ideas for a great headline, what should you do? Look at other profiles on LinkedIn and make one similar but with your own flavor. Does your résumé or presentation on paper show your skills? Of course it does. So what should your résumé have? That's right, your skills. When we list our skills, we will then get endorsed for said skills. This is important.

Make sure all of your past employment information is there. You never know where or how someone will come across your information. That is why you need to make sure you give as much info as you can. Did you attend a college or a university? Just like you would have put that info on your paper résumé, the same goes for your modern day online résumé. What was your major? What was your GPA?

DISCLAIMER: Only put your GPA if it is above 3.0, lol. Actually, 3.5 or higher would probably be better. This is why you won't find my GPA on my profile. Let's not talk about it. It is a sensitive subject for my mom.

In addition to information like the above tips, do not hesitate to give your profile information on organizations you donate your time to, or even charities you raise money or awareness for. I myself have a few on my profile that have to do with ocean preservation, animal welfare, and cancer awareness and prevention. What influences you? What inspires or motivates you? These are the questions to ask yourself when you are completing your resume. Oh, and whatever you do, please make sure you have a nice, professional, high-resolution photo of yourself as your profile picture. In a nutshell, give your profile any and all info you can.

TIP #2: TURN IN YOUR RÉSUMÉ TO THE WORLD

Now that your résumé is complete, it is time for you to get over five hundred connections as soon as possible. Even if the connections are in your same profession or industry, add, add, add. Here is why. Once you get five hundred or more connections, your profile will just show "500+." Now people don't know if you have 501 or 50,000. This way you're evening the playing field. After all, what do you think the consumer is going to think when he or she is referred to you and another competitor of yours, Googles both of you, looks at both of your LinkedIn accounts, and one profile says 132 connections with five endorsements for skills of yours, and your competitors résumé shows 500+ connections with seventy-five endorsements for the same skill? What is the immediate perception to the consumer? One is more connected than the other? One is more successful than the other? One has more experience than the other? Maybe one seems to have a higher level of legitimacy than the other?

As you add professionals to your profile, I want you to think of everyone you can add. Not just people in your industry. Take, for instance, my profession in real estate. The average real estate agent has fewer than three hundred connections on LinkedIn, it seems, and they are all other agents, lenders, escrow officers, title reps, termite inspectors, and home inspectors. I hate to tell you, you aren't going to be getting very much business from those people.

Connections outside of your profession, is the key to higher ROI...

When was, the last time you thought to find all your past and current clients on LinkedIn? Or better yet, even potential clients on LinkedIn. You will be surprised how many people have a LinkedIn profile. Imagine the power of connecting with your clients, endorsing them for what they do for a living, and writing them recommendations on their profiles. For example, a doctor who is a client of mine has been endorsed on his profile from me for heart surgery, emergency medicine, and medical innovation, which is both a nice gesture to give him and deepens our relationship more. Techniques like this have benefitted me time and time again and, even better, have benefited professionals I teach these techniques to every week. Never before in the history of professional networking could it be this easy until the rise of online networks and relationships.

Another great way to connect with people on LinkedIn is joining groups. Some groups are public, and some are private, but there are groups related to almost any profession and industry out there. As a real estate agent in the United States who has both national and international listings, I am a member of various global real estate network groups on LinkedIn. To give you some examples, China

Real Estate Network, UK Real Estate, Luxury Real Estate Network, and The Real Estate Network. You will find that as you join local and global groups, once you start engaging and interacting with other members in the groups, it will lead to building new connections and relationships. I have seen these relationships turn into referrals and leads overnight.

Want to know what groups are even more powerful than that? Well, if you graduated from a university, are you following your university's LinkedIn page? More than likely you are. Now I ask, are you also a member of your university's private official alumni group on LinkedIn? A very small percentage of business people on LinkedIn know that their university has an official alumni group. For example, the University of Southern California (USC) has a few hundred thousand students following the school's LinkedIn page, yet only about fifty thousand are members of the private official alumni group on LinkedIn. So, if you are an alum, put this book down and log in and join your group now. Better yet, if you're reading an e-book, here you go: www.linkedin.com.

I'll wait...☺ (Cue *Jeopardy!* music.)

(*Jeopardy!* music continuing)

When you ask to join one of these groups, the admins will not approve you until they pull up university records and confirm that you are an alumnus. Once they confirm you attended, they approve you, and you become a member. So you cannot join another university's alumni group. Why would this group be so effective and beneficial to you and your business? How would you use this to your advantage? What approach would you take? Over periods of time, I have tracked how effective these groups can be. Think for a moment: who are the people in these groups? A very high percentage of the alumni in these groups are career-driven people. Many of them can also be on the wealthier side of business, especially when we are dealing with the elite universities that are out there. So what is the approach once you're in?

I have noticed that although posting my own content in these groups is effective, what really seems to give return on investment (ROI) is when I like and comment on other people's posts in the group…when I congratulate other fellow Trojans on their successes…when I ask questions for more details or info on a post…when I follow that up with a connection request as well. The first time I saw how the power of this group was when I congratulated someone who posted in the group that she had published her first book. The individual then replied an hour later to me with this:

> "Tony, thank you so much! I sent you a connection request and saw on your profile that you also wrote a

book. I just read the first few pages of your book on Amazon and bought it. I see you also still live in LA and sell real estate? I moved back to NY after I graduated. One of the executives with my company in NY, who attended USC also, just told me he is being transferred to LA, and I know he will be buying a home. I told him I would have you call him. Is that OK?"

Uhhh, yes, please!? That moment was when I also realized what was even more powerful with these alumni groups. Want to know? If you still live and do business in the same area you went to school. Most move back home after they graduate, so the amount of potential referrals to you from fellow alumni who no longer live there is huge. There is no limit on what you can achieve when it comes to building relationships on LinkedIn. This example above has happened so many times to me and to agents or recruiters I mentor. It is not a surprise once you realize a very important fact. What mode are you and most people in, when they are logged in to LinkedIn? Business mode!

TIP #3: INVEST IN YOUR BUSINESS AND CAREER

Remember at the beginning of this chapter, where I stated that when you pay for LinkedIn, you open the doors for more opportunities? Being able to see who has viewed your profile is one of those perks. Now most of you know that this is possible. Some of you probably already pay for LinkedIn and can see everyone who has viewed your profile. However, less than 1 percent of professionals understand why knowing who has viewed your profile could be a great benefit to your business and productivity. There are many reasons it can benefit you, but let's just reveal one of my philosophies on this. When a consumer Googles a professional's name, you will almost always see LinkedIn on the first page of results. Take, for instance, if a client of mine refers a friend to me, what do you think that person is going to do upon receiving my name? Yep, Google me. Among various sites on the first page of results, he or she will also see LinkedIn, which will say something like, "We found 28 profiles with the name Tony Giordano on LinkedIn." When they click that link, it will open the list of all twenty-eight profiles. Want to take a guess who is at the top of that list of all the Tony G's? I am. Why? The reason is that I pay for LinkedIn, which allows me to be at the top of the list in priority. Or in other words, it allows me to be the most important business professional with the name Tony Giordano. I now have made it very easy for the consumer to find me at the top of the list without having to scroll down and review each of them to find the right one. This is yet another great reason to have a premium account on LinkedIn. If information is so easy to access today, shouldn't we, as professionals, be just as easy to access? Yes or yes? ☺ Without a doubt we should.

Let's get back to the example now. My client refers this friend of theirs to me, their friend then Googles me, and potentially looks at my LinkedIn, and after their friend has viewed my Linkedin Profile, I now get what 'notification' from LinkedIn? It notifies me that this person has now viewed my profile. Most do not understand how knowing who has viewed their profile would be beneficial to their business. When I am mentoring professionals who have started a premium account with LinkedIn, I will often pull up the list of people who have viewed their profile. I will ask them who these people are. The majority of the time, the list will be people in their industry, colleagues, clients, and "don't knows." Many times I have heard an agent tell me that a new client is also on the list—someone he or she actually just started working with, or quoting insurance rates to, or just started showing property to, or who just hired his or her law firm, and so on. I am going to share a story in my industry of when I saw a new client on this list of profile viewers while mentoring an agent.

> ME: "Out of these nineteen people who have viewed your profile in the last thirty days—who are they?"
> AGENT: "Realtor, realtor, realtor, don't know, realtor, lender, lender, realtor, my client right now, escrow officer, realtor, termite guy, don't know, realtor, insurance agent, title rep, past client, friend, realtor..."
> ME: "I'm curious, Jason. You said your 'client right now.' Who is she?"
> AGENT: "Husband and wife who were referred to me by a friend. We found them a house last night, and we are going in to escrow today."

ME: "Congratulations on the new escrow! You said she was referred to you by a friend; when did she contact you?"
AGENT: "Let's see…today is Friday, so it was last Wednesday."
ME: "So ten days ago?"
AGENT: "Not even that; last Wednesday for sure, so nine days ago."
ME: "Hmm. Jason, when does it say she viewed your profile?"
AGENT: "Thirteen days ago…wait, what?" (Utter shock)
ME: "She was doing her what?"
AGENT: "Research? It just doesn't make sense? She was referred to me by close friends."
ME: "Jason, it doesn't mean she is not going to Google you. She could have easily been referred to two other agents by other friends she has as well. She may have looked at all three of your websites and LinkedIn profiles. Thank goodness your online résumé was complete. Better yet, thank goodness you are proud of your online résumé."
AGENT: "Very true. You can easily forget that people can research everything before they call you. Even I do it, I need to realize that consumers will do it to me."
ME: "Yes, you do. Now that I have your attention, I have one more question for you. If I had asked you who she was last Tuesday, the day before she called you, what would you have called her in this list?"

AGENT: "A 'don't know.'"
ME: "Jason, you just named two other 'don't knows' in this list of nineteen people. Who are they? Could they be referrals doing their research? What should you do?"
AGENT: "Yeah, they might be. Should I connect with them or send them a message?"
ME: "Sure. What are you going to say?"
AGENT: "I know you looked at my profile?"
ME: "*Wrong!* No one wants to know you know what they are doing. But what if you just sent them a connection request with no message? What if, when they get that message, it makes them think, ***That's strange: the agent whose profile I just looked at yesterday is sending me a connection request today? Oh, you know what, maybe Sara, who referred him to me, told him how to find me on LinkedIn. I should just use him at this point."***

See, maybe by simply sending them a connection request, you stopped their research of other potential agents to use. Maybe you don't send them a connection request on LinkedIn. What if instead, you find them on Facebook and send them a friend request. Now they may think, ***That's strange: the agent whose profile I just looked at yesterday on LinkedIn is sending me a friend request on Facebook today. Oh, you know what, maybe Sara, who referred him to me, told him how to find me on her Facebook. I should just use him at this point.***

You never know who these people are. It never hurts to send a request. Linkedin truly is the number one network when it comes to lead generation and ROI. That is when you use it the right way, versus the way most people use it, which is the wrong way.

NOTES

CHAPTER 8

the #news @pproach

www.twitter.com/tony_giordano

Twitter is the news network. Not a "social" network per se. The power of this platform, still to this day, is incredible. However, you must understand its niche. Whenever I am teaching this topic to an audience, I have them participate in a little exercise at the very beginning. I want you to picture yourself in a room with five hundred people and picture this exercise in your head as I write it below.

EXERCISE

> "Please raise your hand if you have a Twitter account, and keep your hand up, please, until my questions no longer pertain to you. Everybody look around and see how we have about seventy-five percent of the audience with their hands raised. Keep your hand raised if you know your login. Lol. We always lose some hands there. Keep your hand raised if you consistently tweet and are very active on your Twitter account. Everybody continue looking around; as you will see, we just lost about half the hands remaining. Keep your hand up if you have actually captured and closed business that came directly from Twitter. We now have lost almost everyone besides the five hands remaining out of five hundred people."

What is even more amazing to me is how this exercise produces the same results on average every time I do it—which is weekly. About 75 percent of salespeople have a Twitter account, but literally less than half of them are active. Out of the remaining hands up, we lose almost 95 percent of the remaining hands after I ask how many have actually captured and closed business from it. Why? Well, most don't understand Twitter's true best value. Most people use it when they need information. They are watching the news; there is a breaking story you want more info on, so you go to Twitter to get trending media on it. Or you're on the 405 Freeway in Los Angeles (if any of you have ever had the pleasure of that), and traffic is dead-stopped, and it's way worse than normal, so you're wondering what's going on. You're in between off-ramps, wondering if you should exit on the next one. Do you really go on the California Highway Patrol's website and zoom in with your little fingers on your phone to try and see what dispatch calls have come in recently in LA? No, you hop on Twitter, hashtag #405Freeway (or #HELL; both will work for that freeway), and you are going to see, without a doubt, people in the same traffic tweeting a mile ahead of you saying something like:

> "Massive truck overspill on #405Freeway, get off at #Sepulveda Blvd if you can."

...or whatever the case is, and say to yourself in an Austin Powers voice, *"Ah-thank you!"* ☺ Right? You use it when you need info, but other than that, most of you are not active on Twitter. Or some agents may tell me every now and then that they tweet their open houses, but nothing comes out of it. The conclusion to most agents: "Twitter must not serve any other purpose."

Actually, Twitter is incredible. Still to this day. It only gets more incredible, I think. Basic Twitter for those who don't know or didn't read the first edition of this book (shame on you. You should. It's on Amazon. OK, I'll stop now.): The @ symbol is how you talk to another account holder on Twitter. You mention the user with the @ symbol and talk directly to that user. So if you wanted to talk to NAR, the National Association of Realtors, and tell them something so they see it, it's not @nar, it's @nardotrealtor. They actually spelled out dot—don't get me started. So, quick tip, never assume you know what the username is. Many people try to get creative, so it is important you find the right username for the account you are trying to reach. Or maybe you want to reach the official Ted Talks twitter page. It's not @Ted, it's @tedtalks. On Instagram it's @Ted, but on Twitter it's @tedtalks; that's the username. Or @INMANNEWS, the largest real estate news organization in the world. It's not @INMAN, it's @ INMANNEWS. Or @Tony_Giordano is how you would talk directly to me.

As I discussed on Instagram earlier, the # (hashtag)—or, for some of our older ones, the pound sign, or for some of our even older ones, the tick-tac-toe game (lol)—is the topic you're talking about. By adding the hashtag in the front of the word #Malibu, or two words #BeverlyHills, or three or four even, the word becomes the color blue and makes the word "clickable" (like a button) now, so someone could click and find more information on that topic, or find you because he or she was searching for that same information and now sees your tweet in the news feed.

Let's do a basic tweet, so we are all on the same page on the correct way to tweet. Let's just think of something to tweet. Let's say that you were like, "Man, I really wish I could go on Twitter right now and say how great this book is." I'm just using this as an example; I'm not saying you have to do this, I'm just saying we're using this as an example, that's all. ☺ "How would I mention Tony directly so he sees what I said about his book?" Well, it would be @Tony_Giordano. So if you went on Twitter right now, like right now, if you wanted to, that is, and said something like

"@Tony_Giordano's book is blowing my mind on #OnlineMarketing..."

...and then you were wanting to make sure Tony Robbins, TED Talks, or INMAN NEWS saw your tweet too—not saying you do or that you're going to, this is still just an example. Lol. Well you would then continue with something like:

"@Tony_Giordano's book is blowing my mind on #OnlineMarketing. He should do a @TEDTALKS and share the stage with @TonyRobbins @InmanNews."

I'm not sa'ying you're going to do this tweet. I'm just saying if you did, that would be the right way to tweet it. Everybody get that? ☺ So simple recap, where it's easier for you to just copy and paste it if you're reading an e-book is:

> @Tony_Giordano's book is blowing my mind on #OnlineMarketing. He should do a @TEDTALKS and share the stage with @TonyRobbins @InmanNews.

Oh, I already counted the character limit of this tweet to make sure it was under the max character limit Twitter allows in a tweet. Not for any reason besides just showing you the right way to tweet and make it easy for you if you were to copy and paste and felt a need to tweet that. ☺ All right, enough with my jokes. Let's get into what techniques advanced Twitter users do that go much further down the rabbit hole.

THE "GETTING **** DONE" NETWORK

August of 2009 is when I joined Twitter simply because it was blowing up as a massive network and people started using it to capture information and/or news or follow their favorite celebrities. For the first few months, I did nothing with it really. During the months of December of '09 and January of '10, I had been working on a short sale (distressed home sale) that I got from a Facebook friend whom I had added randomly one day in the beginning of November. Bank of America was the bank we were trying to get the approval from, and B of A had both the first lien against the house and the second lien against the house. For over two months, I was working my butt off on this deal to get this short sale approved, and Bank of America finally approves the first loan, and on the same day, it sold the second loan to a collection agency. Like really? How incompetent could the bank be? Sad thing, it happened to many agents and sellers during the 2008 housing and economic crash. They didn't know what one cubicle was doing from the next cubicle. After getting this news, I called B of A, and said, "What just happened?"

I will spare you the very long, detailed story and month-long battle I was facing against both B of A and the collection agency. I did everything I could. I filed complaints with each institution, spoke with executive offices from each institution, filed complaints with the US Treasury and OCC against each institution, and probably went through the same process of trying to explain my point over a hundred times, until, at the end of the forty-five-day battle, I lost. Collection agency was not going to take a dime under $50,000 for the second loan payoff approval, and B of A was not going to extend my approval on the first loan if the collection agency declined that side, and would begin foreclosure process on my clients.

I admitted defeat. There was nothing more I could do, and I had already done ten times the techniques most agents would have done. At this point, I was upset, sad for my clients, and that night I just decided to hop on Twitter, not thinking anything would come out of it. I just went on Twitter and expressed my opinion of B of A in 140 characters or less. That was the character limit on Twitter back then, 140 characters, meaning short and sweet. Now they have it at almost twice that. So you have to learn how to abbreviate and get creative on getting your point across. I really wanted to express my opinion of B of A in about eight characters or less, but I took the high road and chose not to. ☺ I also wanted to make sure Bank of America saw my tweet by mentioning its official blue check mark verified Twitter page. Actual tweet:

> @bofa sells 2nd loan same day they approved the 1st loan!? Now my clients will be forced homeless and on the streets. Shame on #bofa.

Seven minutes later—*seven!*—another user account on Twitter mentioned my user account @Tony_Giordano, and who do you think was mentioning my user account? B of A!

> @BofA Tweet to @Tony_Giordano: "@Tony_Giordano, we saw your tweet. Will you please follow us back so we can DM you."

DM, direct message offline, that nobody can see. So I followed them, even though the last thing I wanted to do was to follow B of A on Twitter, right? I got a DM with them asking me to contact them at the following phone number. I called.

A lady answered and said, "We are the online media department at corporate Bank of America that oversees all online media when it comes to what consumers are saying online, resolving any issues that we can, and/or simply staying in touch with our consumer base. Anything that has to do with B of A online, we watch and respond to here at corporate B of A. We saw your tweet; we are concerned, so please tell us what happened." So I told her the whole story for about thirty-five minutes, only to hear her say this at the end: "Tony, you've done everything you can. I mean the complaints, the US Treasury complaint, the complaint at Realtime, trying to get us to work together. We are sorry. We don't have any tricks or inside pull with the collection company. The B of A executive officers told you the truth. It's not like the collection agency is our company. But would you do me a favor and let me look into this for you, and in the meantime while I am, will you please stop tweeting?"

I calmly responded, "No, I will not stop tweeting. You go do what you have to do, and I'm going to keep doing what I'm doing, because I am sick and tired of your company telling me the words 'Let me look into this for you.'" She understood my frustration, and we ended the call. At that point, I was late for an appointment and rushed to this client's house. About two hours later, I came out of the appointment with a voice mail from her on my phone, and I also saw that I had an e-mail in my inbox from the collection agency. I opened the e-mail, and lo and behold, there was an attached written approval good for sixty days for $6,000. This from the same company we battled for forty-five days that declined it three times, saying it would never take less than $50,000, who also caused B of A to start foreclosure process on my clients? *What is going on here?* I thought to myself. I immediately called this lady back at B of A, and she asked me three simple questions.

BOFA: "Did you get an e-mail from the collection agency?"
ME: "*Yep!*"
BOFA: "Was it what you needed?"
ME: "*Yep!*"
BOFA: "Will you please delete your tweet now?"
ME: "Uhh, *Yep!*"
ME: "I'll make you dinner."

No joke, I could not believe it. I actually went on Twitter and complimented B of A right after saying how I thought it so amazing B of A had that department to begin with. I went back to my office and told my manager what happened. He turned around and has me say that at the sales meeting the next morning at our office in Malibu. Other agents then used this same technique and were successful as well. Eighteen more times in 2010, 2011, and 2012, I had short sales receive a written decline letter from a bank, went on Twitter to express my opinion, and seventeen of the eighteen were resubmitted and approved in the same week. That is powerful and very effective ammo to have in your arsenal, is it not?

Think about that: nineteen times I tried it, and eighteen times it worked. And it wasn't just B of A. It was also @chase, @wellsfargo—they all had the same departments inside their headquarters. My following on twitter in December of '09 was six hundred people—that's it. Just six hundred people following me, which had nothing to do with it working. Bank of America did not want that out there for anyone to see who was searching for information about Bank of America, because now I was going to show up in those searches because I hashtagged it. With the searchability on Twitter today, you don't even need to hashtag for people to find you when they search any words you are using in a tweet.

So many times it does not have a lot to do with your following as much as that the company you are mentioning just does not want it online. Then, after 2012, the US housing market started to rebound and gain steam again, and the short sale (distressed housing market) industry fizzled away, but I knew the technique of mentioning a company online still worked. So I didn't stop there.

> "@Southwest, the incompetence of your flight attendant on #flight1433 is shocking to me. How on earth can you call yourselves the best."

> Minutes later, @Southwest to @Tony_Giordano:

> "@Tony_Giordano please e-mail us at social@southwest.com and explain what's going on, we're concerned of your tweet."

I e-mailed them, and they e-mailed me back. Long story short, two days later, after some back and forth, I get an e-mail from Southwest: "We've credited your account for a free flight anywhere in America. We are very sorry this happened and hope you continue flying Southwest."

But I didn't stop there either. Two and a half months later:

"@Southwest on my way to San Francisco and just met one of the best flight attendants I have ever met."

Minutes later, @southwest "retweets" my tweet this time, of course, lol, and mentions me once again. So this technique is also for complimenting. It is not just a technique used when you need to make a complaint or get something resolved. In addition to that, they retweeted my compliment to their million followers.

"Look what @Tony_Giordano has to say about Southwest. Thanks Tony, enjoy the friendly skies."

...and boom, forty more people followed me that day. Why? Because Southwest just told the world @ Tony_Giordano thank you to their million followers, and a few checked out my profile because they saw Southwest mention my account. Why did they follow me? Because I also have a lot of tweets and valuable content for people. These random people see my profile and think to themselves, *No wonder Southwest and Tony know each other.* (No, we don't.) *Look at this guy: this guy gives valuable information. I'll follow him too.* But they would never decide to follow me if they see I hardly ever tweet, and my account serves them no purpose. That gives them no value. People want value online. Sales is a "what" game? Numbers. I don't care if these random people were on the other side of the globe. What if one day they know someone who needs help selling a home and now think of me to refer to those people? *Numbers*!

So your first key niche of Twitter is the getting "blank" done network. You fill in the blank. Instagram can also be a getting "blank" done network as well now. You show a photo or video of a flight attendant or something going down, and you Instagram share that? Oh yeah, they'll be all over that as well. But Twitter is really the powerful network that gets it to go viral to millions of people and news channels. What is another key niche?

DISCOVER INFORMATION OR GET DISCOVERED

Just like with so many of the other networks we've discussed in this book, I have to have my personal Twitter account, and of course my business Twitter account @opulentagency.

In June of 2010 I was sitting an open house in Beverly Hills, California, up in the hills with a breathtaking view of downtown Los Angeles on the horizon, and as I always did, I went on Facebook and posted a photo of that gorgeous view and said something like:

> Sitting an Open House on a gorgeous day in Beverly Hills. How can I call it work with a view like this? Come see me and have a glass of champagne.

Or something like that. I always posted on Facebook something about my open houses, but I posted in a social way and made it more about the photo than about business. However, that day I remember thinking, *You know what? I've got to start tweeting. I get that I do the short sale tweets and use that technique, but I've got to start tweeting more relevant content about the community, local cities in the area, the real estate market, and if I just posted my open house on Facebook, I should start tweeting these open houses too.*

So I went on Twitter and I just typed almost the same exact description I posted on Facebook, but look for the difference:

> Sitting an #OpenHouse on a gorgeous day in #BeverlyHills. How can I call it work with a view like this? www.TheOpulentAgency.com

That day, I had a contact off my website, and after reaching out to him, I had come to find out it was through my tweet that he ended up on my site. Of course I began doing it all the time after that. Every chance I had to tweet something about the local area or real estate in my area, I did. About one month of consistently tweeting my open houses throughout my areas in Los Angeles later, I was doing an "open" in Santa Monica, California. This property was on the beach. I snapped a stunning photo of the view from the deck overlooking the sand and sapphire-blue ocean on the horizon. Once again, I hopped on Twitter, attached the photo, and typed:

> My office for the day. #OpenHouse on a gorgeous day on #SantaMonica Beach. Love selling #realestate in #LosAngeles. www.TheOpulentAgency.com

This time, a man named Thomas in New York had found out the day before that his company was promoting him and moving him to Los Angeles from New York to become the new executive of the entire western region launch of the corporation. Thomas, coincidently, had lived in Los Angeles for most of his childhood, so he was very pleased he was moving back home. He needed to head to LA that month for the company to start the process of moving there, so the next morning, he hopped on Twitter to…find a real estate agent? No. Nobody uses Twitter for that. He went on to Twitter to get information on what? Yes, Santa Monica. In the search bar of Twitter, he searched the hashtag #SantaMonica, which opened a news feed on Twitter of dozens upon dozens of tweets from tourists, residents, companies, the city of Santa Monica's tweets, restaurants…and all these people were using the hashtag #SantaMonica. Thomas wanted to know what was happening in Santa Monica that weekend because he was coming into town. As he scrolled further and further down, all of a sudden, about a couple dozen tweets down, he sees me come in:

> My office for the day. #OpenHouse on a gorgeous day on #SantaMonica Beach. Love selling #realestate in #LosAngeles. www.TheOpulentAgency.com

...and he just happens to need a real estate agent. He wasn't looking for me. He was looking for information about Santa Monica and happened to find me and happened to need me. Thomas mentioned my account and followed me. I followed him back as he requested, and we DMed each other our contact info. While I was sending him my info, I was also looking him up on LinkedIn, found him quickly, and saw that he was legit and also the company he said he worked for, and so on. We hopped on a call together, he let me know his plans, he flew in to town that weekend, and, long story short, two weeks later, he leased and closed on a beachfront property in Malibu. Didn't purchase a property at first; however, leases make commission too, especially luxury leases. I got a check for $14,845 the day after he closed, and for doing what?

Tweeting? Question to you, though: Would Thomas have found me if I didn't know how to tweet? Probably not. Here's an example of what I mean. What if I had gone on Twitter during my open house and typed,

Sitting an open house on a gorgeous day in #Santa #Monica.

Not quite the same, is it? Is he going to find me? No. Why? Because now I'm only going to be in a news feed and discovered by people looking for information about "Santa" or a really popular girl named Monica. If there are two or even three words of a city or topic, you must conjoin the words as one with the hashtag. Not #New #York #City. The correct way is #NewYorkCity, or #NYC is very popular for that particular city. You also have to think of what hashtags people are actually searching for. Do I care about the hashtag #realestate or #openhouse? Not really. It could be people looking for #realestate or an #openhouse anywhere in the world. It isn't area specific. I'm more concerned about my city names and hashtagging those because I know people are constantly looking for information online about those cities. Think of powerful words in your tweets to hashtag, and you will be good to go.

Oh, and please don't make up your own hashtags thinking that they are brilliant ideas. Boy, do I see some crazy ones out there.

Sitting an Open House in Santa Monica today. #BestRealtorinSantaMonica

Nobody is going on Twitter and searching for that. No couple buying their first home are going on Twitter and typing #BestRealtorinSantaMonica, and clicking search and saying, "Look, I found her, Babe. See, it says it right there, she's the best." Nobody is searching that except the agent who does it to scroll through her own tweets in front of her friends. ☺ Don't get me started on the long sentence hashtags either. These long hashtags you see people creating, they're hilarious to me because they go nowhere, and they do nothing for you. You've all seen it somewhere, or something like it, probably. Instagram too, even. A girl uploads pictures of flowers that her boyfriend got her, and she posts and says something like:

> Just got these beautiful flowers from my man for Valentine's Day. #lovehimbestboyfriendeverIhope-heasksmetomarryhimonedaybecauseiwillsayyes

That's not going anywhere. Unless there is a trending short sentence that millions are using—then maybe, depending on the sentence and topic. Otherwise, keep it to things that actually will help produce some type of a lead, customer, increase to your following, brand awareness, traffic to your website, and/or new relationships.

What we just went over was how to be discovered. After I got that first check, it was on. I was jumping in with both feet on Twitter. Thomas found me because I knew how to tweet and speak this online language. You do now too. Most agents or sales professionals would stop at this technique, though. What do I mean? I mean they wouldn't try to go further and learn more techniques. Most agents would think to themselves, *Wow, I see the power in this, and I am going to keep executing this technique and be found by more people in the world like Thomas who are looking for information on the city I sell real estate in.* You see, they stop right there. Don't get me wrong, I am going to keep tweeting, too, and getting found more and more as well. But I didn't just stop there. I am always trying to figure out how to get more ROI out of something. Especially as a coach and speaker, I want to find out all the ways I can get a return on my efforts in these platforms, so I can also turn around and teach it, which is my passion. But I also want to raise the ROI any way I can because I am a businessman and need to make money. After getting that check from Thomas's closing, I had to ask myself great questions, as I always say. How did this work? Why did this work? What exactly worked? Who else can I get? My actual thought process in my head was this:

> How did I get discovered? Thomas discovered me because he was discovering information about Santa Monica. And of course I will keep doing these same tweets and be found by other people too. But if he was discovering information about Santa Monica and found me, what would stop me from discovering information about Santa Monica and see if I could find people in Twitter using the words Santa Monica, and maybe find people moving here?

I then went to the top search bar of Twitter and typed these words in exactly like this:

Moving to Santa Monica

Just like that, a normal sentence, "Moving to Santa Monica." Once I typed it in, I clicked the search button, and ladies and gentlemen, Twitter pulled up every single person on the face of Planet Earth who had recently tweeted the words, "Moving to Santa Monica." These people were in other major cities, countries, and even locally in Los Angeles. What did you just say, Tony? You read it right. Even better than just seeing a hundred tweets of people who had tweeted that, I could reply to all of them on their tweets:

Welcome to #SantaMonica. Local expert and resource on housing, restaurants, schools and services. www.TheOpulentAgency.com

For every ten to twenty replies that I sent out, three, four, sometimes half would respond and say thank you or ask for more information. I was also able to track contacts off my website who came from Twitter in my websites analytic charts. Oh, and who cares if someone didn't need a home—what am I now to them? That's right, a value and resource to them. Do you think I stopped there, though? No I didn't. I started to type and search the entire areas where I sell real estate. Moving to Beverly Hills. Moving to Malibu. Moving to Westwood. Now, if you are as proactive as I am, I already know what you are doing. You are trying it on Twitter right now. Go ahead. You will be shocked with what you see. It's just out there, ladies and gentlemen. I don't think we realize, out of billions of people on Earth, how many millions upon millions tweet or express themselves online in ways we just wouldn't think to search. It's crazy how easy it is now to go out there and find them. We do not have to wait for the phone to ring anymore. We can simply go online and search people using certain words and find them before they even start looking. We went from being discovered for our business and brand to now also discovering people for our business and brand.

Chapter 11 will go into online advertising and marketing. Twitter has an advertising platform, and what you learn in chapter 11 when I use Facebook's ads platform, you can also do on Twitter. So we won't get in to that in this chapter.

NOTES

CHAPTER 9

the "SEO" approach

www.google.com/+tonygiordano

By now, most people know what "SEO" is—search engine optimization. In a nutshell, it is your visibility online and how you show up in results organically when people are searching for you or what you do for a living. There are several search engines, and they all have different ways they target and track SEO. No reason to go over other search engines, because we all know at this point, there is only one. *The one!* Yes, we are talking about Google. If you don't think Google is number one and the best, I will give you a few hundred billion reasons why they are. Simple, it is their worth. But, for the sake of your time, here is one fact we know on why they are the best:

> Dear Yahoo,
> We have never heard anyone say, "I don't know, just 'Yahoo' it..."
> Sincerely,
> Google

It's simple. Google is the largest search engine in the world. Now, once you realize this fact, the question is: Do you support everything Google?

We will answer that question later in this chapter. First let's discuss the social aspect, Google+, which has been nicknamed (and remained) the "dark horse" of the social networks. I was saying it even when they first came on the scene. If they do not figure out a niche, they will fail, and in just a few years, they ultimately failed with their initial attempt to compete, primarily because they couldn't figure out their niche in order to compete with Facebook, Twitter, LinkedIn, and so on. Why did this $300 billion company of Google even want to launch a social network? They're Google.

Well, do you remember a few years ago when you would search for a person or place on Facebook, and there would be a little drop down menu where Facebook would try and assist you with your search? For example, if you were to search Tony Giordano, it would say,

People named Tony Giordano
Places named Tony Giordano
Groups named Tony Giordano

and right at the very bottom, Facebook began showing,

Web results with Tony Giordano

Guess who those web results are powered by? No, not Google. Facebook powered its web results through Bing. Need I say more? Let's break this down. If there are well over a billion people on Facebook all the time, every day, searching for topics and clicking on the web results as well, then think about what Google saw in the distance. I will tell you what they saw. They saw a search engine named Bing go from nothing, to #10 in the world, to #9, #8, #7, #6, (skip a few) and boom, #2, second-largest search engine in the world. So imagine Google seeing this search engine climbing the charts out of nowhere and being fueled even faster by Facebook search integration. Now some of you may know that technically YouTube is the second-largest search engine in the world, but as it is owned by Google, it's actually Bing that holds the number-two spot for search engine website classification. What was Google going to do about this? There was no way it was going to allow a social network like Facebook to raise up another search engine giant and take them from the number-one spot. That began Google's plan to set out and rise against the big social networks, and it wasn't quiet about it either. We could all hear Google coming from a mile away, preaching its action plan, which in my opinion sounded like this at the time:

> We are going to launch the greatest social network mankind has ever seen. We are going to take everything you hate about Facebook and Twitter and not have it in our network called Google+, and we are going to have circles, rainbows, and crayon symbols to make it easy…

I remember all the posts and media you would see every day on Facebook and other networks when Google announced its new social network called Google+. People and experts were even saying it was "the end of Facebook as we know it." You don't mess with Google. Facebook and Twitter are done. I would literally go onstage at a tech conference right after some expert said that and say the opposite: "Not only are Facebook and Twitter not done, Google+ will fail in less than five years unless they figure out a niche. They don't have a niche." Unfortunately here was Google+'s thought process, and here is my thought process. I am also pretty sure my thought process is the same as everyone's when it comes or actually came to Google+.

GOOGLE+: "Yes, we do have a niche. We are going to be the greatest social network."
ME: "I have Facebook for that. They own that niche."
GOOGLE+: "OK, well maybe we could be a news network because people Google the news."
ME: "I have Twitter for that. You're not going to take the news from Twitter. You're not going to take the little blue bird floating at the bottom of my TV screen when I am watching breaking news. Sorry, Twitter owns the news."
GOOGLE+: "Well, we own YouTube, so we'll be the video network. We'll, pair the YouTube channel and the Google+ profile together and so people can watch YouTube videos on their Google+ profiles."
ME: "I know you own YouTube, but people prefer to watch videos on YouTube."
GOOGLE+: "OK, well, we will be an interest network."
ME: "I have Pinterest for that. They dominate the social network twist when it comes to retail, products, interests..."
GOOGLE+: "How about the photo network?"
ME: "Yeah, once again, I have Instagram for that."

People said I was crazy to be stating onstage at conferences that Google+ would fail on some level, no matter what. Finally, thank goodness, they did. Google announced the official dismantle and failure of Google+. It has already began shifting its approach and plan and how it will attempt to keep Google+ in some way of existence, because it knows it has to have some level of social media inside Google. But it is no longer trying to compete with Facebook as a global social network. This does not mean you delete your Google+. Also, if you do not have one, you need to launch one because you need to be ready for the transition of whatever Google is planning. Google doesn't care about Facebook anymore. It finally figured out its niche: wait a second, we're Google. If you don't support everything Google, then we won't support you, and we're just going to go ahead and keep you on page 2 or 3 of results when somebody Googles your name. We are the largest search engine in the world by millions more than anyone combined, and you need to be all in with Google if you want us to show you in Google results. Why? Because we know people aren't Yahooing or Binging you at a high level. We know they're Googling you, and we don't owe you anything, so you'd better support us. Do you have to pay? Not necessarily; you just have to be active on everything Google.

So its niche that puts it in the top five of all online media, which you need to have presence within, is that it is "the SEO network." Hence the name of the chapter. That's why you have to be extremely active with Google. Do you think I care at all where I show results on Yahoo or Bing? Not as much as I care how I show in results in Google. That is certain. I am going to support the platform that I know most are using to find me. How do I support it?

DO YOU SUPPORT EVERYTHING GOOGLE?

I hope so, because guess what? Google knows if you do. So you'd better. How does it know if you do? All devices have an address that makes the device's activity trackable. So once any device of yours clicks on something Google owns, Google owns you. Meaning now Google owns you or your device, if you will. By the way, if you think you own a device that hasn't clicked on something Google owns, you are very likely mistaken. Trust me, it has. You will be surprised at the companies that Google owns or how it attaches itself to so many sites. Just YouTube alone—your device has probably watched a video, and Google owns it. Once it owns my device, now it can track how much I support Google. You see, Google now knows if my device has Google set as the default search engine.

> GOOGLE: Tony has us set as the default search engine; give him some love in organic results. Oh, but he logs into Google search engine with an sbcglobal.net e-mail, not our Gmail; take him down in results. No, Tony has a Gmail account as well; bump him up in results. Oh, but he comes to Google search engine through another default web browser, not our web browser Google Chrome. Bump him down in results. No, Tony uses Google Chrome as his default web browser; bump him up in results. Oh, but he does not have an active Google+ profile; bump him down in results.

> No, he does have an active Google+, and he's ready for the transition to the new profile that we do eventually. Bump him up even more in results; he supports us greatly.

That being said, you *must* be active on Google+. It is not that difficult to post something on Facebook and open Google+ real quick and copy and paste the same post in there and post it. You just need to remember to do so. There are so many management systems today to make posting easy for you. The last thing you should be stressing about is adding another network to it. Make it easy on yourself. OK, back to Google.

> GOOGLE: Oh, but he does not have an active YouTube channel with videos of market updates, listings, lifestyle videos that he consistently uploads. Bump him down in results. No, he does have a very active YouTube channel with videos he uploads. Tony understands the importance of video marketing and the number-one aspect we at Google say will help your SEO, which is video. Give him even more organic SEO. Oh, but his business is not a red pin location on Google Maps and does not have a business profile with Google reviews. Bump him down in results. No, he is a red pin location on Google Maps with Google reviews. Bump him up.

Now I know what you might be asking yourself right now, "Well, Tony, how do I become a red pin location on Google Maps, Mr. Know-It-All?"

Google it ☺

That's what I did and simply followed the steps I found right there on the first page of Google. I Google and YouTube everything. Of course, there are a dozen more ways we can support Google even more. Google Earth, Google TV, Google Voice, Google Drive, Google Radio, and so on and so on. Bottom line: support it.

SEO VERSUS SEM

You don't pay for SEO. If you pay for SEO, it becomes SEM, search engine marketing. I could write an entire book about SEM. There are many pros and cons with it. If done correctly, it can be incredible. If done poorly, it will give you nothing. Example of why it doesn't work? Think of the last hundred searches you did on Google. Out of all those searches, how many times did you choose the result at the very top that was an ad, paid for to be at the top? More than likely, out of one hundred, you clicked a top ad on Google results once. What did you usually click on? You scrolled right below those three ads at the top and clicked on the link that earned the spot there organically. Why? Because they earned that position. That means the link has had many people go to the website, and obviously that is more important to people than clicking on the ones that pay to be at the top. However, when you start getting into advanced SEM, you can see some major advantages to it. For the sake of time, and the fact that I teach it in more advanced coaching sessions with students of mine, just go on YouTube and search "geo-fencing on Google." You're welcome.

THE POWER OF ORGANIC SEO

I am going to conclude this chapter with a story of mine that shocks a lot of audiences I share it with. In October of 2009, when I joined Coldwell Banker in Malibu, there was another agent in that exact same branch office who was also a firefighter. We're both firefighters, and we're both real estate agents and in the same office. Kind of odd, would you say? Sure. How about if I go further and tell you that both of our names are Tony Giordano? No relation either. No, I am not kidding. Not at all, actually. Pretty crazy, right? That would be crazy if there were two men with the common name of John Smith who were both firefighters, both real estate agents, and in the same office.

Actually, I already knew him. We were good friends by 2009. I had met him back in 2000 when I was a firefighter in LA County and was giving a speech about Malibu Canyon fires to a group of residents. Someone spoke up and told me about this other man named Tony Giordano and ended up introducing us. It was like looking into a mirror in forty years when I met him. At the time he was in his early seventies and looked just like me; no joke. When I joined the office, they had to start calling him "Tony Senior" and me "Tony Junior." He had been with CB in Malibu for thirty-plus years. I was only with CB for twenty-six months. If you Google Tony Giordano, I dominate the first page of Google results still to this day. But even if you were trying to go further and get him, so you Googled "Tony Giordano Coldwell Banker," guess who still dominates the first page of Google results? I do. Even though I was only there for twenty-six months, and he's been there for thirty-plus years. Why? Because I'm more active online than he is. I am more active with my website and all my networks such as LinkedIn and Facebook, all of which say, "Previous employer, Coldwell Banker." By being as active as I am on all of those sites and networks, my content is constantly firing with those names attached and new data, which builds my SEO. How could this be a huge advantage to me and a huge disadvantage for "Tony Senior"? Guess how many phone calls I get every month to see his real estate listings? I would never take a customer from him, and I quickly know if they were trying to reach him for one of his listings.

Really, I am just sharing this is to show you a prime example of online presence versus present online. Who has presence in this scenario? Who is more accessible to the client? Who easily searchable? Tony Senior only had one line on the first page of results, which was a nonmobile-friendly templated website that looked like a hundred thousand other agents' sites. However, my Facebook, my Twitter, my YouTube videos, my custom website, and everything else was right there. What did we say at the beginning of this book?

"If the information is at their fingertips so they can access it any time they want to find a home (Zillow), then shouldn't you be just as easy to access once they need you?"

Yes, and that takes online presence and an audience that grows every day. This example about Tony Giordano Senior reminds me of a funny story that happened about a year ago. A friend of mine named Mark called me up.

> MARK: "Tony, I was just on another call and thought I was talking to you. I was calling on one of your listings, I thought, but did you know there's another agent named Tony Giordano selling real estate in the Greater Los Angeles area?"
> ME: "Yes, I know, Mark; he's like a grandpa to my kids now. We're really good friends."
> MARK: "Really? That's weird; he didn't sound like he was retiring soon. But anyway, it's just so odd to me."
> ME: "I know it's odd because it's an odd name, and we're both real estate agents in Malibu."
> MARK: "Malibu? He's not in Malibu."
> ME: "Yeah, he's in Malibu."
> MARK: "No, no, no, this guy has only been in the business for a couple of years. He even said he knew who you were and has been wanting to talk to you. I told him you would call him today. Here is his number."

Don't even say what I think you are about to say, Tony. There is no way there is a third one. I couldn't even believe this. I remember thinking in my head, *There is no way!* I called the phone number that my friend Mark gave me, and some guy answers.

TONY #3: "This is Tony."
ME: "Hey, Tony, this is Tony Giordano. Mark wanted me to give you a call. I guess your name might be Tony Giordano too?"
TONY #3: "Ah, the great Tony Giordano. I've been wanting to talk to you for a couple of years. You're the reason I will never be on the first page of Google when I Google my name."

Yes, there are three of us! I can't make this stuff up. Don't believe me? Google it. Realtors in Murrieta, California: Tony and Krystle Giordano. Well, of course Tony #3 had no idea that there was even another Tony Giordano in Malibu. So the conversation went on.

ME: You will never believe this, Tony, but there's actually a third one of us, and he sells real estate too."
TONY #3: "No way. This is crazy!"
ME: "Yeah, he lives in Malibu; he's like a grandpa to my kids, but the funny thing about him and me is not only are we both real estate agents, he and I are also firefighters."

Long pause on the call. His next words out of his mouth:

TONY #3: "I'm a captain with the San Bernardino Fire Department."

I know if you are reading this you are in disbelief, but I am not even kind of kidding. No joke. Why did I share this story with you? The power of online presence and organic SEO, that is why. They've switched everything over to his wife's name for their brand, Chrystal Giordano, because he knows he's never getting past my SEO with this name. So be active everywhere you can.

NOTES

CHAPTER 10

the "channel" approach

www.youtube.com/tonygiordano

We learned about some aspects of video marketing in the chapter on Instagram. With YouTube, though, there are various factors that make it a critical platform to integrate in your business. Just the fact that they are owned by Google, is probably the most important factor. Make sure you have a YouTube channel. If you don't, you must launch one. You must start integrating video into your business. There are many systems out there that can make video marketing and integration much easier for you. Send a video out to your database on a weekly or at least monthly basis. When your clients open your e-mail, they will see the thumbnail and a video ready to press play and watch a quick update or tip from you. There are also apps for smartphones that make shooting video and editing video easier and very low cost, if not free. **Always search what the best apps are online** and that also have the best reviews.

Here's an example of what video editing apps can do. I hire a photographer to shoot a new listing of mine; he sends me all the photos once edited, and I save the photos to my phone and now open the video edit app. When I am inside the app, I can see all the photos that are in my phone's camera roll. I scroll to the photos of my listing that I want to use in the video. Maybe I want to use a picture of the kitchen, bathroom, front yard, backyard, pool, appliances, the local elementary school in the neighborhood, the closest restaurant, a welcome to "City" name sign that I took a picture of on my phone as well...and boom, ready to go. I'm standing in front of my listing in let's say Brentwood, Los Angeles.

I click "Start Recording" or have someone hold my phone and record me. Lights, camera, action. "Hi, everybody, Tony Giordano here on location of my new listing. We're going to be hitting the market this Saturday. As you can see, it's pretty amazing. We're going to be shooting a lifestyle video here today. But let me give you a quick sneak peek. As you can see, the kitchen has just been completely remodeled." (Tap the photo of the kitchen, and now that's all they see, and I'm just narrating.) "But if you think the kitchen is nice, wait till you see the swimming pool. This swimming pool was just built less than six months ago..." (Blah, blah, blah, blah.) "Brentwood is known for restaurants like Baltaire, Katsuya..." (I tap and show pictures of the restaurants.) "And the local elementary school is Kenter Elementary school." At any point I can tap the screen and put the camera back on my face and conclude, "Thank you for watching the video. Call me for a private showing. It will hit the market this weekend."

Like everything, there is an art to this, so the more you practice, the better. If done very well, people will literally think you spent a few hundred dollars creating this video. This is a great way to start integrating video marketing by downloading these apps and starting to become familiar with them from your tablet and/or your smartphone.

FULL PRODUCTION LIFESTYLE OR BRAND VIDEOS

We just went over the inexpensive way of integrating video marketing. But not all video promotions get to be a low-cost production. When is it important to spend some money and shoot something high-quality, do you think? The simple answer: when it deserves it. If I am standing in front of a multimillion-dollar luxury real estate listing with my iPhone and shoot a video like we just discussed, that is OK, because it was just an announcement of more to come, if you remember. In the video I said we were shooting the lifestyle video that day. What is the difference? There is only one way to sell a lifestyle. You can't sell a lifestyle in marketing remarks or a written description. You can't sell a lifestyle in photos or a virtual reality tour. You can only sell a lifestyle through a video. A lifestyle video sells not just what it's like to live in the home, but also what it's like to pull into the garage in a luxury automobile. It sells the viewer what it is like to play with the children in the backyard and walk down to the boat dock on the property and sail away. It sells what it is like to live in the neighborhood and maybe what it is like to attend the local private school. It sells what it's like to live in that city and visit the closest shopping and dining areas. A lifestyle video sells a lifestyle.

https://youtu.be/F21AxWsao9E

and every home is different; which means different music, and overall different feel,

https://youtu.be/x9qRSKt-FRI

The lifestyle videos we shoot are going to be a full-production, high-quality video promoting our client's listings and towns. If you are up for a listing presentation and are going head to head with an agent who can show sellers these types of videos as they have done on other listings, and you don't have these to show, it is not going to turn out very well. Sellers will choose an agent who is planning on shooting a high-quality video over another agent in heartbeat.

These lifestyle videos we have shot for as low as $1,500 and as high as $15,000. All of them are almost the same quality and look just as great. Why the large spread? It depends on where you live, actually. In Los Angeles I am going to spend way more on a lifestyle video than I will spend on one in an area outside of Atlanta. It all depends on what the market for a videographer there is. How do I know? I market listings all over the world, not just LA. The Opulent Agency is in many luxury real estate markets. You will need to do your own research in your area for videographers. Some tips when you are choosing whom you will hire:

- ☐ Have videographers send you listing videos they have shot, edited, and completed.
- ☐ Make sure they are so good at it that you won't need to spend time helping them edit the video.
- ☐ Make sure they send you the file of the video so you can upload it yourself in your name or brand. Don't share your videographer's YouTube or Vimeo links.
- ☐ Never let videographers upload it to YouTube or Vimeo until it is fully edited, approved, and completed. This way no one else can watch it before it is done. Your videographer should only be sharing with you until you approve it.
- ☐ Try to find someone who does everything, meaning photos of the listing, video of the listing, drone photography and videography, editing, graphics in video, and music for video. It's not easy to find an all-in-one who is really good on all those levels, so if you do, you scored!
- ☐ If you shoot a lifestyle video that is over a minute in duration, or even two or three minutes, remember you will need to make sure you have your videographer give you a sixty second version of the same video so you can upload it to Instagram, which allows for only sixty seconds or less.
- ☐ Here is an example of finding a video media company that does all this above. One of the companies we

use, are named Tri-Blend Media, founded by a very good friend of mine, Blake Richards. This is an example of a sixty second version that allows us to upload to Instagram, and of course an example of what finding a great video media company can do for you.
www.instagram.com/p/BfH0zBAnFct/

DEATH OF THE BLOG—BIRTH OF THE VLOG

Am I willing to state that blogging is dead? Yes, I am, and for a couple of years already too. Does it still work? Sure. What I mean when I say it is dead is compared to vlogging. A vlog is a blog using video as the way to get your message or content out. When most people think of a blog, it is usually an online article written through Wordpress or a site. When compared against each other, vlogging has already killed blogging in the sense of effectiveness. Here is an example of what I mean and an example of what I have been sharing to people for a few years already, actually. Let's take two real estate agents.

Agent Blogger: Agent writes an amazing blog titled "Miami Real Estate Market 2017." In this one- to two-page blog, she shares many key points of the local market in Miami and surrounding areas. The agent also shares median home prices, schools, and local resources. In the article the agent also hyperlinks certain words or phrases that you can click on, and it takes you to another article just about that topic. Click-through links work very well for SEO. Attached to this blog, the agent also has keywords and phrases linked to the article for keyword tracking and Google SEO. Article is launched and goes live.

Agent Vlogger: Agent grabs a video camera, whether a phone, webcam, or professional video camera, and speaks into the camera about the Miami real estate market in 2017. This agent also shares into the camera median home prices, surrounding areas, schools, and local resources. The agent also has hyperlinks placed on the video when they upload it that people can click on the actual thumbnail screen while they watch the video. The agent titles the video "Miami Real Estate Market 2017," uploads the video to YouTube, attaches keywords or phrases on that backside of the video for keyword tracking and Google SEO, clicks "Publish" on YouTube, and it goes live.

About a week after both of these market updates have been online, someone opens Google and searches Miami Real Estate Market. Who do you think Google puts in front? What do you think Google prefers when it comes to SEO? You got it, video. Why? What does Google own?

YouTube. Do I have professionals whom I coach who still blog and have yet to switch to vlogging? Yes, I do. Does it still work for them? Yes, it does. However, all of them tell me it does not work at the same level it used to. They also say they do not get the same ROI they once did.

There are several ways to vlog, whether through streaming video, through a podcast, which I use SoundCloud, and although it is mostly audio podcasts, we feed our SoundCloud channel in to our website which also helps with our SEO. http://www.giordano.global/podcasts

You can also vlog live, through the live video streaming feature on various platforms; but in all honesty, YouTube, as long as it is partnered with Google, I just don't think there is a better place to vlog. There are so many videos on YouTube, both on learning how to vlog and how to vlog on YouTube itself. Now we know the importance by this point with integrating video in our business, I hope. Turning this knowledge into action, though, is not that easy for many. The second they are told to start rolling, they become a deer in the headlights when they stare at that camera lens. Let me see if I can have a dear friend of mine help you with this.

"LIGHTS CAMERA ACTION—TAKE TWENTY-SIX"?

Camera is rolling—now what? Last thing you want when integrating video is taking all day and multiple "takes" all the time to get it right. Sandra Dee Robinson is a well-known actress, TV personality, radio host, spokesperson, wildlife advocate, and the CEO/founder of Charisma on Camera, and Charismatic Cowgirl. www.charismaticcowgirl.com

Sandra Dee is under great demand as a coach and consultant to entrepreneurs, authors, celebrities, and experts to help them develop unfailing confidence in their personal presence, both on camera and off. She has appeared in major roles on shows like *Another World, Sunset Beach, The Bold and the Beautiful, General Hospital,* and *Days of Our Lives,* and she has guest starred on many prime-time shows and films. She is driven to empower her clients with the knowledge of the incredible gifts God has given them so they may get their message out and make the impact in the world they are destined to make. So I asked her to write you a little free coaching session right in this chapter from her own words to you directly. Sandra Dee, take it away.

LOOK & FEEL LIKE A ROCKSTAR ON VIDEO

A lot of brilliant people are facing a common problem. Despite knowing that video and TV will increase recognition and revenue in their business, they are getting stuck when they have the chance to get in front of a camera and really connect with their audience. I always hear the same statements, "I don't know how to say what I need to say." Or, "I know my stuff, but can't remember my script." The most common, "I hate the way I look on camera."

The thing is, when we enjoy being on camera, it's much more inviting for viewers to connect emotionally. This is extremely important, because humans make decisions, even business decisions, from the area of the brain that processes emotion. So, it is crucial to understand how to relax and formulate a message, creating this type of connection in the first few seconds of a video or TV opportunity. How do you do this?

First: Address Any Fear

This shows up as butterflies, forgetfulness, and negative self-talk, most people have a fish-out-of-water feeling. This will undermine your effectiveness, so I suggest you make friends with your fear. Notice I do not recommend trying to get rid of fear, because that is an exercise in futility. Fear is not bad. Think of it as a part of you that is programmed to protect you. So picture that part, thank it, and mindfully place it in the back seat. Fear will be along for the ride, but if you safely put in its place, you now direct your energy forward and drive your message through the lens, to exactly the person who needs it the most. Keep your thoughts on your mission and what you are giving.

Second: Video Is a Private Conversation

Even if there are a million viewers, they are each watching one at a time. The more specific you can get picturing exactly who you are talking to, and what you have to offer them, the more personal your message will seem.

Third: Formulate with Stories and Passion

Formulate your message using stories and passion. Stories help us to build relationships. The first stories we were told in life were usually told to us by those (our parents) that loved us. They are a great way to build rapport, show that you "get" your viewer's problem or issue, and build trust with them. Warning: This may require some vulnerability. Don't hesitate to let us know why you are passionate about your product or service. I recommend working with a coach, because as Les Brown is known to say, "You can't see the picture when you are in the frame." Most people have some great "nuggets" in their history that they are not currently using in their message, but they are too close to recognize them.

Along with your ability to connect emotionally with your energy and message, there are some practical tips for creating a great video:

1. *Frame yourself well. Your eyes should be at the bottom of the top third of the screen. That's where we look to connect with you. Place the top of the camera frame at the top of your head for close framing and web cams.*
2. *Make sure we can hear you. Buy an exterior microphone or a lavaliere and shoot in a controlled environment. Planning a shoot in your garden with your camera's built-in microphone is a sure way to invite the neighbor to start up his leaf blower.*

3. *Light your eyes. Face the brightest source of light. If you are placing lights, try to eliminate shadows and aim for the level of your eyes. We connect with your eyes so the easier it is to see them, the better.*
4. *Keep distractions out of your background. What is your background saying about you? Viewers notice.*

Your video camera is the most powerful tool for building your business. We are a society hungry for visual information and entertainment, so feed your audience confidently with your story and be shoot-savvy. The world is waiting for the impact you are destined to make."
—Sandra Dee Robinson

Please give a big thank-you to Sandra Dee. What is even more amazing is that this is only a fraction of what she coaches professionals on. I will go a little further and add a couple extra tips for you.

1. Wear dark colors, as the camera captures you better, and overall, the video looks better to the viewer.
2. If you are shooting a video where you are trying to make it seem it was not all shot the same day, then make sure you have different clothes to change into.
3. Looking away from the camera as if you are being interviewed accomplishes two main aspects. For those who are camera shy about looking into a

lens, that will help. Also, when you look away from the camera, it raises reputability or legitimacy, if you will.

4. Don't act like a costar of your own life when the camera starts rolling. You need to be the lead role of your life and brand. Be the star you are.

NOT BRINGING YOU BACK FOR SEASON 2

With all this advice in this chapter, your video or videos came out spectacular. You nailed your scripts. You looked natural. The videographer you hired shot and edited your video perfectly. In all honesty, you have one of the best promo videos ever shot. You uploaded it to YouTube and the world, and no one watched it, besides those 426 views you have on YouTube six months later. What happened? If no one watches a new show on TV, what happens? No second season, right?

The point of this section is that just because you are shooting great videos does not mean anyone is going to watch them. You now need to know how to get them to go viral. You don't have to have millions of views, but most certainly you want thousands of views. Many people do not know how to upload videos correctly—or shall we say, effectively. Did you know that once you watch a video on YouTube from your phone, it will never be able to count as a view again on that video? This is why you can't upload a video and just keep clicking replay, over and over again, to get your view count up to ten thousand views.

Unfortunately, it does not work like that. The reason is that Google tracks the device address, like we discussed. Every device has an address. So if my Mac, iPad, and iPhone watch a video on YouTube, they count as three views on that video. If all three of my devices watch that same video ten more times each, they will not count as thirty more views. So when you see a video that has one thousand views, that means one thousand different devices have watched it. Doesn't matter how many times each device has watched it. Each one can only count as a view once.

So the most views I can get on my own videos of my business is about seven. Why? Because I only have seven devices in my house that I can personally watch the video on. Any other views I get now will need to be from other devices that belong to other people. This is why, on average, a real estate agent gets four hundred views on his or her videos. Your bigger agents maybe get about twelve hundred views on average that I track. Why? Often they don't know all the different ways that help a video go viral, per se. Here are some tips that will help you get more views:

- ☐ The title of your video is most important. Think of words to title your video that people search for.
- ☐ Description of your video should be detailed. I often tell agents to write the same description that they put in the marketing remarks for the property.
- ☐ YouTube allows you to attach a few keywords to your video that no one can see that will help your video be found when people are searching certain words.

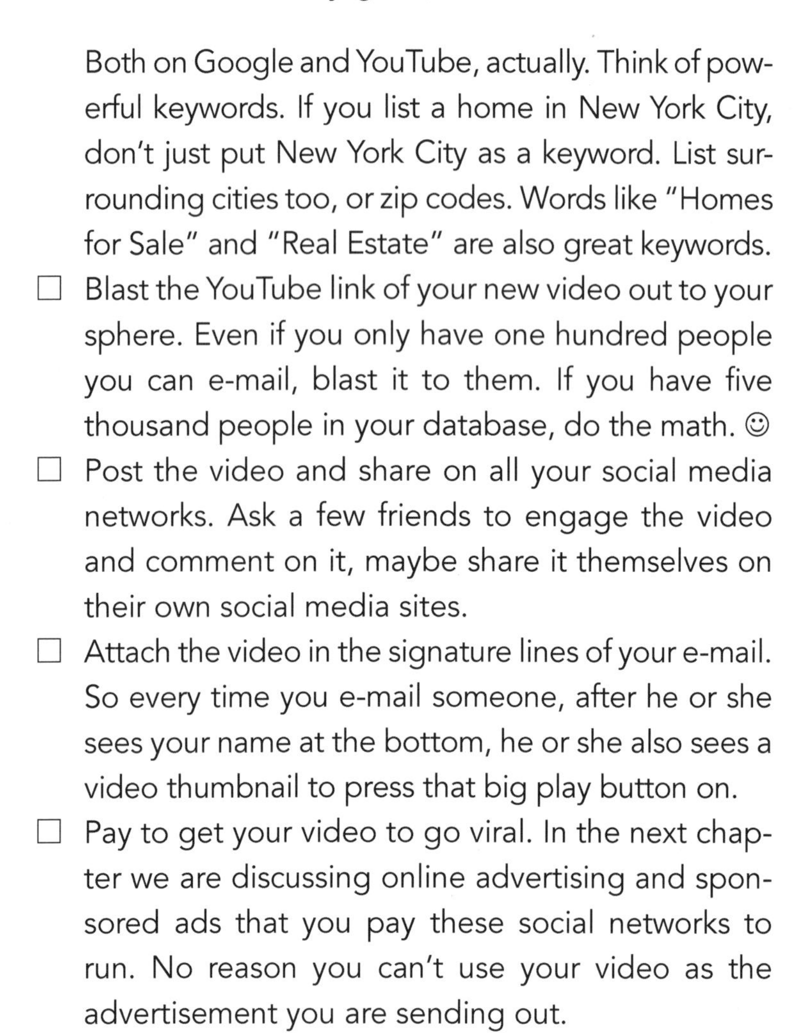

Both on Google and YouTube, actually. Think of powerful keywords. If you list a home in New York City, don't just put New York City as a keyword. List surrounding cities too, or zip codes. Words like "Homes for Sale" and "Real Estate" are also great keywords.

☐ Blast the YouTube link of your new video out to your sphere. Even if you only have one hundred people you can e-mail, blast it to them. If you have five thousand people in your database, do the math. ☺

☐ Post the video and share on all your social media networks. Ask a few friends to engage the video and comment on it, maybe share it themselves on their own social media sites.

☐ Attach the video in the signature lines of your e-mail. So every time you e-mail someone, after he or she sees your name at the bottom, he or she also sees a video thumbnail to press that big play button on.

☐ Pay to get your video to go viral. In the next chapter we are discussing online advertising and sponsored ads that you pay these social networks to run. No reason you can't use your video as the advertisement you are sending out.

As I said in the first edition of *the social agent* years ago, if you need to learn something, *ask* YouTube. This book is to mainly tell you *why* and *what* to do, with some *how* to do as well. However, everything I learn *how* to do is almost always on YouTube when it comes to this world of online presence. Get in the habit of asking YouTube.

NOTES

CHAPTER 11

the "targeting" approach

www.facebook.com/giordanointl

In this chapter I'd like to spend some quality time on marketing, advertising, and targeting online. We are going to mainly use the Facebook business page in this chapter as the example. However, what I teach you in this chapter, you can do on most of these networks in some way or another when it comes to advertising online. There are really only two ways your Facebook business page can be very effective with extraordinary results—not kind of effective with moderate results. I mean extraordinarily effective, where your brand, productivity, and profit grow consistently. One of these two strategies must happen with you, or it will never be extraordinary for your business.

One, Oprah calls you and invites you on to come on a special show of hers as a guest, where she will be interviewing you in front of millions watching that morning, and while you and she are talking, at the bottom of the TV screen, it shows the millions of viewers your Facebook URL to follow you, and organically, that morning, tens of tens of thousands do end up following you. So, that's one way for your Facebook business page to become greatly effective for your business. ☺

But if that one strategy never happens for you, the only other way for your page to be greatly effective is if you pay for it. Period. Begging your friends and family to go like your business page and maybe a couple hundred others who have organically followed your page over the last couple years is not going to give you any extraordinary growth. This is why, on average, a salesperson or small business has five hundred likes on his or her business page, and it's all his or her closest friends, family, and a few clients whom he or she begged to go like it.

To open this chapter, I am going to run you through the same thing I do in front of audiences, and it is almost always the same response and same percentages with the outcome. For this example, we will take an audience of one thousand to keep the math and percentages simple to grasp. As you read this, picture the actual audience from the stage participating.

Today, if I ask an audience of one thousand to raise their hands if they have a Facebook business page, 850 on average raise their hands. When I ask them to keep their hand up if they are active on their business page, I lose about 250 hands, so I am quickly down to only about 60 percent of salespeople and small business owners who feel they have active business pages. As their hands stay raised in the air, if I ask them to keep their hands up if they know what the button "Boost" and/or "Promote" does on their business page, I lose another three hundred people on average. Now we are down to 30 percent of people who know what those buttons can do. Out of the three hundred or so hands remaining up, I will then ask them to keep their hands up if they have spent money and actually paid Facebook and boosted and/or promoted their pages. After I ask that, I lose another hundred hands, taking us down to about 20 percent of salespeople and/or small business owners who have actually done it on some level. To my final two hundred or so hands remaining up, I then ask them if they have a monthly budget set aside and run campaigns consistently each month. Now I lose about 100 to 150 more hands, taking me down to only about 5 to 10 percent on average of people who are running consistent online campaigns for their brand. That is a shocking stat to me, when we know big business rakes it in with online advertising. Want my final question to the audience, where I see if I can get it to drop even more?

> "For the fifty to one hundred hands remaining up out of the thousand people here, keep your hands up if you actually receive consistent business from your online efforts and these campaigns."

No joke, out of the fifty to one hundred hands that remained, I lose almost all of them and am usually down to about ten to twenty hands max. Out of one thousand? Literally 1 to 2 percent of salespeople and/or small business owners are reaping the rewards of this modern-day form of advertising and marketing. No matter where I do this exercise, it is the same on average and is the national stat. I have yet to really see it go up in percentage. It's crazy to me. I've been literally revealing these techniques for years and hoping to see more and more people reap the rewards of it. Yet it stays pretty much at the same percentages. I get so upset—or passionate, if you will—because there's nothing else like it, and it works one hundred times better than any other forms of offline advertising, and it is a fraction of the cost of offline advertising. There's unbelievable potential ROI on this.

THERE IS AN ART TO EVERYTHING

Less than 2 percent of sales professionals understand the art to boosting and promoting, which is also known as demographic targeting or even "specific targeting," if you will. You're forcing your brand promotion or boost in front of the online news feeds of certain demographics you have chosen or selected to target. As you get more experienced, you will start to see the ROI increase when you ask yourself great questions so you can really narrow down and be purposeful with whom you will target.

The Great Questions

1.) **WHOM** do I want to target?
2.) **WHY** am I targeting them?
3.) **WHAT** content am I targeting them with?
4.) **WHERE** do I want to target these people?
5.) **HOW** am I going to get ROI out of it?

You really have to ask yourself great questions to truly know whom you are targeting and why. Let's discuss the PROMOTE strategy first.

PROMOTE PAGE, WEBSITE, LOCAL BUSINESS

When you're logged into your business page on Facebook, you then have the ability to promote your actual page, or your website, and force your page as a sponsored ad into anyone's newsfeed whom you target. This is a very effective way to build your brand awareness if done correctly and, even more so, build your following. What do I mean by "correctly"? Here is an example of the power of demographic targeting and promoting your page. This is just one example. My luxury real estate Facebook business page is called the Opulent Agency, www.facebook.com/theopulentagency.

I can literally run a promotion and force my real estate page in front of a specific audience I choose. If I am a real estate agent, then whom would I want to try and get to follow and like my business page? Well, remember the great questions we need to ask ourselves? So as I ask myself these questions, here is the audience I am going to choose as a real estate agent. First, Facebook's ads manager is going to ask me to choose

Gender: Men, women, or both

For this campaign, I am going to choose both. Next option is going to be

Age:

Of course it depends on what you are trying to promote at times. As a real estate agent, I may want to stay in the homeownership age group of mid- to late twenties and go as high as sixty-five-plus years of age. For the sake of this example, I will say thirty years of age to sixty-five-plus years of age as my demographic. Next option is:

Location:

Where do I want to promote my page as a local business? That's right, locally. Now, I run campaigns nationally and internationally with my brand. However, it is because we are also in those other cities and countries. But we have many business pages that are local for those particular areas. In this example, let's just take the Opulent Agency's Los Angeles page. For location, I will of course choose one of my local cities or zip codes. How about Beverly Hills? Great. I choose Beverly Hills, and now it will let me choose a narrow or broad mile radius around Beverly Hills. If I am trying to build my brand to local people thinking of buying or selling real estate, then I probably won't go beyond a twenty-five-mile radius to Beverly Hills for this particular campaign. Next option:

Interests:

What interests do I want this audience to have? I am a real estate agent and brand, so I of course would want this ad to draw traffic of people who might be buying or selling a home soon. For this example, let's take sellers as the ones I would prefer to attract to my page. What interests do homeowners and potential sellers have? At this point, when I am coaching someone or speaking to an audience, I start to hear people say that interests of homeowners would be shopping, golfing, hiking, boating, schools, and so on. But remember, there is an art to this. Renters and/or people who will never own a home love and show interests in those same things too. What interests could I name where I know I am at least dealing with homeowners? I am sure your mind is racing with ideas, and I am sure some of the interests you are thinking about are very good. Home Depot? Lowes? Gardening? HGTV? All great interests as well. Go deeper, though, I mean really deep. Dive down that online rabbit hole in your head right now. Put yourself in a homeowner's mind-set. If I own a home, and I am thinking of selling soon, what interests might I be clicking on my devices? At this point, you may be one of the very elite few who rarely guess the interests I choose. Are you ready?

Zillow, Trulia, Redfin.

Now, is that brilliance? Nope. It's common sense. It's logical, and that is the reason most don't think about those interests—because we overthink and look right past the logic. We make this world of online marketing and social media marketing way more complicated than it is. *Stop it!* ☺ The more you take the time to learn how to execute these strategies online, the better you will get at it. Or make sure you hire someone or a company who knows how to correctly do it for you. Back to the example now: we have named our interests above, and you can also *exclude* certain demographics from seeing your campaign. Who would I, as a real estate agent, want to *exclude* from seeing my campaign where I am trying to target homeowners? I think you probably guessed it: other real estate agents. ☺ Once you have chosen all these options and narrowed in on the demographic you are going to target with your brand, now it is time to cough up the dough and hand your money to Facebook to do the rest. You pick your budget. No need to break the bank. For this example, if I choose to run this ad for ten dollars a day, for a period of ten days, totaling $100, Facebook will tell me, right where I put the amount in, how many people who fit that demographic that they estimate will like my page every day while the campaign runs. If they estimate ten to twenty-five new people a day will now be following my business page, that would be one hundred to two hundred and fifty new likes to my page by the end of the ten-day campaign. I don't care if it was one person who liked my page. I know he or she lives around Beverly Hills, is over the age of thirty, and has been showing interest online related to either Zillow, Trulia, or Redfin, or showing interest on all three together even.

WHAT IS 'CHOOSING AN INTEREST'?

When you list an interest, it means that per Facebook algorithms, the device (smart phone, tablet, laptop, desktop, etc...) that the user has been using while logged into Facebook, has also had activity clicking on websites, links and/or ads related to the interests you are choosing. You have all seen this, especially you ladies You click on a pair of high heels, and now whatever website you go to, you can't get away from those same exact high heels. They are literally haunting you, right? It is called digital remarketing, and because your device clicked on it, the advertiser can now target you more.

Retargeting

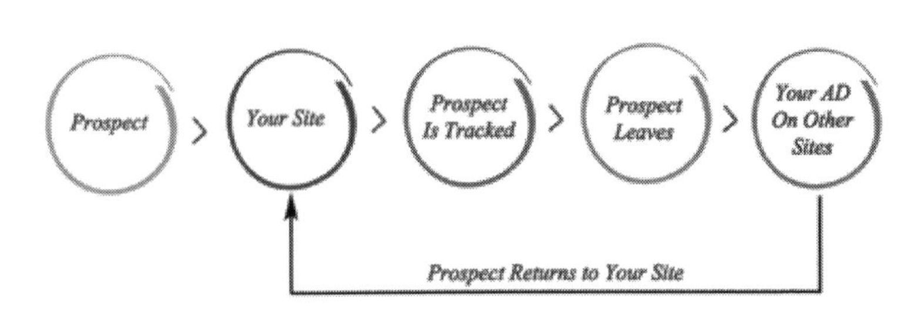

Now these techniques can be very advanced and way more effective as you get advanced. That is where I try and teach people great strategies here, and the extraordinary techniques come with time as you learn this, and even more so with coaching and consulting. So that's some of the strategy and techniques of how you promote your page or website effectively and force your brand in front of an audience to engage and follow your page or website or local business...

BOOST A PARTICULAR POST ON YOUR PAGE

The "boost" button you will see on an actual post you have shared on your page is to promote the actual post, not just your page. The button usually can be found at the bottom of your post and is very easy to see. Or of course you can go into the ads manager and boosts posts from there. "Boost" is very similar to "promote" when going through the steps of choosing the demographic you are going to target and force the post in front of. However, like with everything, there is an art to promoting, and a different art to boosting. Both need to be mastered. Let's first use a real estate post for an example of boosting. I want you to picture a gorgeous beachfront home, and the photo I post is an image of a stunning infinity pool of turquoise-colored water pouring into the beautiful sapphire blue Pacific Ocean under a sunny blue gorgeous sky in Malibu, California. Put yourself there and picture that photo in your head right now. This is a brand-new listing of ours for $22,000,000 that we are getting ready to sell.

(Hey you, wake up! I said just picture the photo. I didn't stay stop reading because now you're in a daze thinking of vacationing in Malibu. Snap out of it. Are you back? OK, good. Where was I?)

Oh yes, the photo of the stunning swimming pool. As an agent my job is obviously to sell this home for my clients. So before I start marketing this property and knowing whom to target, I need to ask myself a few of the great questions again, right? Let's tweak them a bit, though, for this example. It starts with the most important question, "Who is my buyer?" Meaning, who would actually buy this home. Here we go on targeting and advertising our post of this gorgeous home with the infinity pool.

The Great Questions

1.) **WHO** are the buyers I want to target?
Who can purchase a $22,000,000 home? Is it an executive buyer? Is it a celebrity, or an athlete? Is it a family home? Is it a local buyer? Is he or she out of the area? Out of the country? Could my buyer be both a local person, and/or international person? If potentially both, that means I should run a boost campaign and try to find a local buyer, and it also means that I should run a completely different boost campaign and try to find an international buyer. Why two separate campaigns and not just run one and mention local cities and global cities?

Because the demographic and the interests they have will be different. So the best way to target each of these potential buyers is to run separate campaigns.

2.) **WHY** are they the buyers I need to target?
Is it a certain style home that only certain nationalities love? Is it the home of a single man or woman who is an athlete or executive with no family, so he or she doesn't really care about yard space or schools?

3.) **WHAT** content should I target them with?
If they are local, will they recognize the beach name in my post? If they are international, could I talk to them directly and even write hello in their foreign language?

4.) **WHERE** do I want to target these people?
If I run the local campaign, how many miles should I run as a radius? How many miles would they be willing to commute to work from Malibu? Or is this a vacation home? If international, where? Meaning, what country should I target? Or better yet, countries? Is there a trend? Are there certain countries that purchase Malibu beachfront properties more than others? Yes there are, and it is my job as an agent to do my own research and to know what countries those are—which I do. ☺

5.) **HOW** am I going to get ROI out of it?
This is a very important question, if not the most important. How do I draw traffic to this listing and

> know that the people I am targeting will engage the post and like, comment, or "contact us" on our website? What kind of follow-up should I be prepared to execute? Will I need to make a follow-up plan and decide what to send them as the follow-up? The answers to all these questions are yes!

In this scenario let me run you through the same steps for both potential buyers at the same time to save you and me both time. Click boost, and start choosing your demographic. First up, gender.

Gender: Men, women, or both

For this campaign and almost any campaign, I am going to choose both. The next option is going to be

Age:

What is the age of the buyer more than likely? If they are a local wealthy person, are they as young as forty? Thirty-five? Thirty? Have we ever heard of the term "trust-fund baby"? So could or should we target over the age of twenty, even? If we are running the international campaign, is the demographic usually older than the local demographic? Almost always, yes. But be careful making that conclusion without doing your research first, because every area and market is different in its own unique ways. Next option is

Location:

Local radius for this Malibu beachfront estate is going to be twenty-five miles tops. At least for me, anyway. If we are trying to find an out-of-the-area buyer in another major city or state in America, then I may just list the zip codes or cities of the most common US cities or countries who purchase Malibu or Los Angeles real estate, and place fifty-mile radiuses on each of them. Next option:

Interests:

If local buyers, what interests do I want them to have where I know I am getting my listing in front of local people thinking of purchasing real estate? Or better yet, Malibu beachfront real estate? Don't start saying the other interests we ruled out before: boating, beach living, kayaking, shopping, schools, and so on. What did we say before? Yes:

Zillow, Trulia, Redfin.

What other interests could we target for our local potential buyer? Probably many actually. Do we need to besides those interests, though, is the question? How about our out-of-area or international buyer? What interests do I want someone in Saudi Arabia to have if I want to force my listing in front of them to potentially buy it? Or people in New York City I may target? Or Chicago? Or China? What would I want those people to have as activity on their devices? Is it the same yet again?

Zillow? Trulia? Redfin?

No, it is not the same this time. See, out-of-area people, or international people, could be showing interest in Zillow for their own local areas. This means I want out-of-area people that I am targeting to be showing interest on their devices on only one thing:

Malibu, California.

This means the city or area my listing is in. Is your mind spinning with ideas now? Did I just unlock Pandora's Box for you? Can I ask you a favor off topic? Could you call it Giordano's Box? I am trying to build a legacy. It would mean a lot. Thanks. ☺ OK, back on topic, do you see how the interests would change depending on who or why you are targeting a certain demographic and specific audience? Think about it: if I am thirty-five years old, living in Saudi Arabia, and my devices have been clicking on links and apps related to Malibu, California, recently, do you think I am probably going there soon? Do you think I might know someone from my country who will be going there soon? Do you think I know someone in Saudi Arabia who already bought a home there maybe? Ladies and gentlemen, I can't even begin to tell you the power that this level of marketing has today. Before this digital world, the closest ability to demographically target was if I listed a horse ranch for sale, and I ran a full-page print ad in *Equestrian Magazine*, so I knew I was at least marketing it to people who obviously love horses and read that magazine. The problem with that, though, is the magazine I am running the ad in won't tell me how many people saw it, watched it, clicked it, tagged it, viewed it, shared it, liked it, or commented on it. They won't tell me where they live, how old they are, and what interests they have. Why? Because they can't track it either. Now we can, in the modern-day magazines and mailboxes today, the social networks. Oh and not only do I have all that information, I also have all the information of anyone who saw it, watched it, clicked it, tagged it, viewed it, shared it, liked it, or commented on it: where they work, job title, where they live, family, vacations, and so on. This is a level of marketing that no other form of marketing and advertising can compare to. Imagine how powerful this would be to sellers when you are sitting down with them, and showing them you know how to execute this level of marketing. That is why knowing how to do it will benefit you greatly, but that is just one aspect to how this can benefit you. There are several other pillars that will capture even more ROI that I teach in my coaching.

RAVING FANS CREATE THE "FRENZY"

The more your posts are engaged, the more the domino effect will keep progressing. Facebook will always push highly engaged posts in priority of lower-engaged posts. There are several companies out there that can help with this and create raving fans. I have researched and beta tested many of these platforms, and one that I have found does an outstanding job is a company called Rally App at www.rallyre.com/frenzy18. By the way, that link is a promo link that offers special promos and/or discounts. Rally is a multi-industry platform that connects with your social network pages and creates content that on average gets much higher engagement than most content. I call it "Filler Content," which is bonus content they are posting on your behalf in addition to the content you or your team and company is posting. Although there are many companies who do this, they are the only one that also runs campaigns for you, and receives the permissions from Facebook to capture the IDs and contact information of the people who engage your posts. If that's not enough, Rally then has a streamline process of entering these people into a database in their system dedicated to you that will allow you then to "target" them on another round of digital remarketing. Here is an overall recap of Rally App:

- ☐ Posts content on your behalf
- ☐ Creates the "Frenzy" of High Engagement
- ☐ Builds Raving Fans of your brand
- ☐ Runs targeted sponsored and promoted campaigns
- ☐ Captures contact info of engaged account holders
- ☐ Builds your database for retargeting campaigns
- ☐ Gives you *all-access*

In other words, they are leverage you really can't put a price on. However, I left the best part out. This leverage can cost as low as only ninety-nine dollars a month for a small business with a company like Rally App.

To illustrate this a bit further, some of the largest Fortune 500 companies and brands in the world market their brands this way, and on a much larger scale than what we just discussed. Big brands will hire an influencer marketing and technology company, like Influential, to run an online campaign for a new product they are releasing. Influential uses an AI influencer technology that matches brands and influencers through transparent data and machine learning. The company was founded by friends of mine, Chris and Ryan Detert, who are innovators in the industry. They understand how to execute this level of marketing for very large corporations and brands with worldwide presence. These campaigns can cost these brands hundreds of thousands of dollars, if not millions. As an example, let's take Coca-Cola. Influential will launch a massive global campaign with influencers and create a frenzy of engagement from millions of consumers online, who will start raving about Coca-Cola's newest product, which, in turn, creates FOMO (fear of missing out), and only makes other people want to try it. This is where, once again, the domino effect of engagement begins, and if the campaign is executed correctly, it becomes unstoppable. But don't just take it from me. Here's what one of the founders explained. "At Influential, we look to identify the perfect influencer for any campaign by matching them to a particular brand, using our three major precepts—demographic, contextual, and psychographic data," said Chris Detert, Chief Communications Officer of Influential. "With demographic data, we're finding information like age, gender, geographic region, and affinities. Then we look for contextual information—things like 'Does the influencer talk about the brand itself or proxies of the brand?' Lastly, and most importantly, we use AI to read both the influencer's and brand's social media accounts to identify psychographics (personality characteristics) that the influencer and the brand have in common. These are traits like 'adventurousness,' 'extroversion,' 'artistic interests,' 'altruism,' and even 'hedonism.' In our experience, matching influencers and brands based upon demographic, contextual, and psychographic data leads to as much as 30 percent higher engagement on FTC compliant (#Ad, #Sponsored) social media posts."

Pretty great, right? Give it up for Mr. Chris Detert. If the big brands get to do this, and see its constant return on investment, shouldn't you be able to for your business and brand as well? To put it simply, which is better, raving about yourself to your audience, or someone else raving about you to an audience? Of course we all know this: it is when others rave about us that our productivity significantly increases. Rally App has figured out how to do the same thing Influential Inc. does for the big brands, but for you personally, your small business, the real estate broker, the insurance broker, the financial broker, the retail broker, the retail store, the private practice, the recruiter, the salesperson, the entrepreneur...

NOTES

CHAPTER 12

the "mobile" approach

The more we become a mobile society, the more we need to know how to execute all these strategies and tasks from our mobile devices. When I say all these strategies, I mean *all* of them we've been discussing. Communicating, texting, instant messaging, face-timing, meeting people, building relationships, deepening relationships, social selling, branding, advertising, paying bills, booking reservations, booking flights, boarding flights, shopping, buying products, ordering transportation, ordering food, buying groceries, ordering medicine, ordering mobile doctors, mobile services, mobile resources...UBER this, UBER that, UBER need, UBER want, UBER now, LYFT me, LYFT her, LYFT them, LYFT us, LYFT when. Right? The younger the generation, the more common this has become.

COMMUNICATION AT ITS BEST

The younger the generation, the more mobile they are and will be in the future. I think it's funny when I hear people saying, "It's so sad to see these younger generations more interested in their technology than going outside." My sons are always on their devices; however, my oldest son Michael also has a 4.0 GPA in school and can pretty much play any sport there is with a ball. Everything must come with balance, though. My youngest son Christopher has autism, yet when he is on his iPad, he is in another world. He is literally building worlds at those moments he's deep within his tech. It has already been scientifically proven that a child's brain is firing a thousand more times a second within these technologies, than when I was a child playing outside, staring at the mud, with my Tonka Truck in my hand, wishing it was one of the toys where the little doors and hood opened. Yeah, not a whole lot firing in my brain waves at that moment. Lol.

You can't forget that this generation grew up with technology. They grew up with a device in their hand the same day they were given a bottle or a sippy cup practically. It is in many ways an additional limb to their human body. Many would rather lose their sense of smell than their technology. More than likely even you reading this book right now can't live without your technology. What do you do when you can't find your phone? That's right, you turn into a ninja, don't you? You will levitate and float across a room in a split second, while looking at all your surroundings, until you find that device. You will take out anyone in your way while doing it too. Let's go a little further: I have often said that our phone chargers are the modern-day umbilical cords. They are our lifelines today. This may shock you, but if I was asked today:

> SOCIETY: "Tony, you have to make a choice. Choose between the one of the two for the remainder of your life. Either your technology or your pinky finger?"
> ME: "Will it hurt?"
> SOCIETY: "Probably, yeah."
> ME: "Here is my pinky; take the left one if you can. Be gentle, please."

Why? My technology is a greater value to my life. Not just from a business standpoint, but from a learning standpoint too. It's also the way I can stay in touch with my family and friends at a high level too. It really is everything today. We are way more dependent on our technology than we are on our pinky finger. At least I am, anyway. I don't know about you, but personally I do turn into a ninja when I realize I can't find my phone. I could even be in midconversation with a friend of mine, but the moment I can't find my phone, *my ears will start ringing as my brain fades out and deepens my friend's voice like a bomb just went off. An immediate adrenaline rush kicks my heart-rate up 1,000 percent, with all other senses going on high alert, as I become a SWAT officer frisking every inch of my own body, my pockets, slapping my chest, butt, legs, all while floating like a butterfly across my living room at the same time, and seeing everything in slow motion as I observe my surroundings, just to realize that only two seconds have gone by since I lost my phone, and it's in my other hand.* Then real life comes back, and I am wondering how I got to that side of the living room and why I am standing on a table. ☺

If you don't agree with me that even you are just as dependent on your technology as I am, then close your eyes and picture this for a moment. You arrive at a busy airport. You still have to claim your baggage, and you have a call scheduled with a client you have to take once you are past TSA. As you stand in line, you get a text from your family that they need you to call them as well. Your plane takes off in thirty-seven minutes. At that moment you see that your phone is at 3 percent, and you also realize that you forgot your phone charger. Now did I get your heart rate and dependency on your technology to increase? More than likely. If I didn't, then I am going to guess you are retired, or not running a business day to day. Someone else is running it for you.

When an older generation thinks about a younger generation, unfortunately many times, the older generation looks down at them. They may even poke fun at them. Often this is because they simply do not understand what these younger generations have grown up with. I can also say that the older a generation is, the less they rely or need their technology. What do I mean? They are using their technology and smartphones today for what we were using them for fifteen to twenty years ago. Most of the older demographic is barely looking at photos, taking pictures, or even texting. Yet younger generations and I have been using smartphones in that way for twenty years. That is why you will hear older generations saying toward younger generations, "Why are you always on your phone? What could you be doing that is so important?" Maybe there is a younger couple at dinner on a date, and an older couple staring at them because they are both on their phones for ten minutes not even looking at each other, so they think the younger couple cares more about their technology than each other. Most likely it is because the older generation assumes they must be looking at photos, playing a game, or texting some other people, because what else could they really be doing? Little do they know the young couple is reviewing the proposal from the wedding planner that was sent to both of them via the Docusign App, and one of them is searching on Google to see if they can add something to the proposal, while the other reviews each item and the pricing on the proposal. Not only is the young couple not ignoring each other, they are super happy, and after reviewing the proposal, what looks to the older demographic like the young couple are each playing a game of fruit ninja, and completely ignoring each other, is actually both of them signing the wedding proposal electronically with their fingers.

I know kids who have homework on iPads, yet it looks like they are just playing. Bottom line: we are a mobile society today, and the older the generation, the less they understand it. The question is, regardless of your age, are you mobile? Are you making sure you consistently adapt with technology in your business today? Are you making yourself accessible in multiple ways online and in communication? The younger generation is the future of your business. They are the next college graduates, business professionals, doctors, attorneys, business owners, sales professionals, and more importantly, homebuyers and home sellers. This generation today only communicates in two ways: texting and/or social media.

Oh, and what generation are we referring to? What do we call them? "Millennials," right? Well, don't call them that. They hate that word for the most part, mostly because of the negative connotation that comes with it. You will hear older generations making statements that "Millennials" are lazy, ungrateful, and only care about their technology; they have this feeling that they are owed, and/or should be given everything. Now this may be the case for some "Millennials" and people in all generations, actually. However, the majority of "Millennials" are not. This is the most brilliant generation of human beings that have ever walked the Earth. They too have grown up with a device in their hand and information being thrown at them from a hundred different angles. They have so much information thrown at them every minute that they actually have what I call the 90/10 Brain. It is a therory of mine that many of them have agreed with. In short, it is for every one hundred bits of information that come their way, they quickly have to filter in their mind if the information is of value and qualifies for the 10 percent they are willing to listen to, accept, and retain in their mind. If not, they quickly filter and identify the information as the 90 percent they let go in one ear and out the other. It's not that they aren't paying attention to you; it's that it's just not falling into the 10 percent they are willing to retain and absorb. They also can make decisions in a fraction of a second, and it's amazing how their brains are able to solve or come to those decisions. They don't have time to interview three real estate agents in their living room for ninety minutes each. They can make that decision in minutes on their mobile devices. Here's an example:

> "MILLENNIAL": "Let's see, real estate agent John has five reviews with a perfect score of 5.0, 5 for 5 stars. Real estate agent Jennifer has thirty-two reviews averaging a 4.84 score rating. Jennifer it is!"
> Done. Decision made. Why did they go with Jennifer?
> "MILLENNIAL": "There is no way Jennifer would have thirty-two reviews averaging 4.84 if she wasn't great at her job. John, although perfect, only has 5 reviews, two of which have the same last name (Mom and Dad). I'm going with Jennifer."

You think they are fast in that scenario? You should see them when they want to leave a bad review. Or when they are hungry. ☺ They are the future to your business and success. They are your future clients and many of your clients already. They are also your competitors coming into your business, who will take your business very quickly if you are not evolving with the digital times. If you are a businessperson who still wants longevity in your career, you must adapt and integrate this world of online media, communication, and the mobile way of life into your business today.

SOCIAL NETWORKING MEETS SOCIAL MESSAGING

In recent years the rise of social-messaging platforms has become part of the global online world. What is social messaging? It is a social network and/or app that is designed mostly for communicating, whether locally with friends and family, or globally with anyone. However, it is better considered, "texting on steroids." There are many social messaging apps out there, but two are very widely known: WhatsApp and WeChat.

WhatsApp Stats

- ☐ Over a billion active users globally
- ☐ Over sixty languages
- ☐ Over fifty billion messages sent a day
- ☐ Over a billion video messages sent a day

If you have had to deal with a foreign national for your business, or simply have friends and family who live internationally, then I am almost positive you already know about these apps. WhatsApp is the most popular globally and has well over a billion people using it. They are owned by Facebook as well, which many are not aware of. So once again, you can see the dominance of Facebook and how they continue to innovate for their consumer base.

WeChat Stats

- ☐ Over a billion active users globally
- ☐ Majority of users are in China
- ☐ 90 percent+ of China's major city populations use WeChat
- ☐ Over 80 percent of WeChat users purchase products through their WeChat App

WeChat is very similar to WhatsApp. However, it is mostly popular throughout Asian countries. WeChat also has a much stronger social network side to it than just social messaging. I have been able to meet and build new relationships that have become clients of mine inside WeChat from a couple different countries in Asia, including China, Japan, and Singapore. Tencent, the current owners of WeChat, also have a pretty large interest holding in SnapChat, so we could also see a merger there possibly or it has already happened by the time you are reading this.

Both WhatsApp and WeChat are extremely important to have and use, and they are where the next evolution of communication will evolve. Everything we do today continues to become more and more ideal to do from our mobile devices. Even using the big social networks. We navigate on them from our phones way more than from our desktops. Here are some tips to help you through the craziness.

MAKE IT EASY ON YOURSELF

All the big social networks need to be on your phone. You need to group them all together in an app group on your screen so it's easy to get to them. You can even name the group "PERFECT 10," or SOCI@L, or even "Tony's Crazy Group" or something. ☺

TIP:
Create an account on each one. Once you have an account, I want you to log in to each app, and guess what? Never log out. Make it easy on yourself to be able to open the apps and rapid-fire post across the board. Facebook post, rapid-fire, copy-paste post. Open Twitter, copy-paste, add a hashtag, tweet. Open Google, copy-paste, post. Why never log out? So you don't need to play the username and password game, forget password, reset password, wait for it to e-mail you, reset password, relog in, and then forget what you

were even doing in the first place. Always stay logged in to the apps, so that it's easy for you to rapid fire through them, whether posting, liking, commenting, replying, surfing, checking your notifications, or anything else you do when you are inside the online world.

There are many videos on YouTube where you can learn the mobile aspects to these social platforms and navigation techniques. Eventually everything that I taught you in this book you will have to learn and know how to execute from a mobile device. That will eventually be the only way we even use these online sites. Instagram is the best example for where this world is going. Everything we do on Instagram is through the mobile app. Your mobile device today is a part of your human body. Add GPS and location settings to this, and it is definitely a part of your human body. I remember a few years ago in Japan there was a dating site that had a mobile app, and it was the first to use devices in this manner and take advantage of the fact they have GPS and location settings. If two people who were on the dating site looking for their match happened to also be in the same coffee shop, the dating app would alert the user and notify him or her that someone on the same site who was a match happened to be standing ten feet away, and it would show the photo of the individual. That was a few years ago. Now this is a common feature and growing in popularity on various platforms. You may have seen this if you have these settings enabled in your apps. You walk into a restaurant, and the Facebook app tells you that your friend is there too. Or a client of yours or a past acquaintance.

"THERE'S AN APP FOR THAT"

There's an app for what? How about an app for everything? I just say there is an app for life itself now. So much of what I do every day is done on my phone. Apps that allow me to sign documents, order services, send money, receive money, do billing or accounting, create tools, scan documents, connect with people, build relationships, play, grow, learn, teach, create videos and photos, market, advertise, offer virtual assistance, artificial intelligence, and bots assistance (Google it), along hundreds of more things. In all honesty, ***what these apps allow you to do for free on your own used to cost thousands of dollars if you had to hire someone to do them.*** I have no idea what people were doing years ago without the technology of today and coming tomorrow.

Here is the key point to all of it too: those who are willing to always be learning based and adapt to new forms of technology, communication, or systems always dominate more in business than their competition will. I see it every day with professionals whom I coach. By the time the competition realizes the importance of a new form of technology or leverage, a younger generation has already taken some of their business. Oh, and they did it from their fingertips on a mobile device too. We must always be willing to adapt, not just for our own selves, but even more importantly for our clients. I know there are so many tools out there today and mobile apps that make it hard to decide which one is the best or the one you should learn. If you take the time to do your research, though, and always look at the reviews and ratings of the apps, you will eventually find the one that is the most popular or seems to be the best and easiest to use.

NOTES

CHAPTER 13

DEATH of the 'COLD' CALL

Oh, I said it, and it is a fact. It is also the title of my multi-industry book: *The* DEATH *of the* COLD CALL. The reality is simple. There are two certainties with this: either agree that the death of the cold call has happened, or keep cold calling, and it will be the death of you—meaning, the death of your business. First, let me define a cold call. In any industry, I (or anyone who is a salesperson) call a random number, someone picks up the phone on the other side that I don't know at all, and I start my pitch. Or I knock on some random front door of a house, and the door opens, and someone I don't know, whom I have never met, says hello, and I begin my cold pitch. That is why they call it a "cold" call. There is no knowledge of any connection or relation or similar interest with that person yet.

In real estate we know the term "expireds," right? Calling an "expired" isn't cold calling. It is right above cold, because I know they want to sell. So even that is better than cold calling. We can call expireds "room temperature" calling. But cold calling is just that: cold. You are starting to talk to someone and connect with them from scratch with zero knowledge of who they are or if they have any interest in what you have to sell. With everything you just learned in this book, why on earth would you ever choose to "cold" call, when today we have all this information online at our fingertips to make "cold" calling warm? Actually, boiling hot. Forget cold calling, I'm "hot connecting." (My term; you can use it.) I, or you reading this with a little coaching, can do in thirty minutes online what it would take well over a week to do in any other form of lead-generation or prospecting. Fact and proven.

You know when you go on Facebook and see little thumbnail photos of people with a little green dot floating by their name? Meaning they are online, right? Who is online? A human is online, that's who. That's a human being on the other end of that green dot. Let's just take my industry as a real estate agent for a moment. Imagine if you could go door knocking and see a green dot on the front door; you'd know that somebody's home. Next house has a gray dot; they're not home. What doors would you knock on? Green ones, of course, but why? They're home, that's why. There is a conversation behind the green-dot door, and conversations lead to business. You will have now raised the quality of your lead generation. Why? Because now you can just go to the green-dot homes where you know the door will open, but then when you see a house that has a gray dot, they're not home; you can just run up to the porch and drop your business card, or your refrigerator magnet, or your little bag of sand and seashells, or whatever it is that you do to rise above your competitors, and then move on to the next house. You don't have to stand there for two minutes knocking on the door only to realize they're not home. Now multiply that by fifteen houses that weren't home, and already a half of an hour of your lead generation has been wasted standing on a porch because nobody was home. But a green dot on the door—no more wasting time. Higher ROI, higher quality—but that doesn't exist while door knocking, does it? Or any other form of lead generation, for that matter. Imagine if you could go to the homes with the green dot, and right before you knocked on the door, the front door had writing on it that stated:

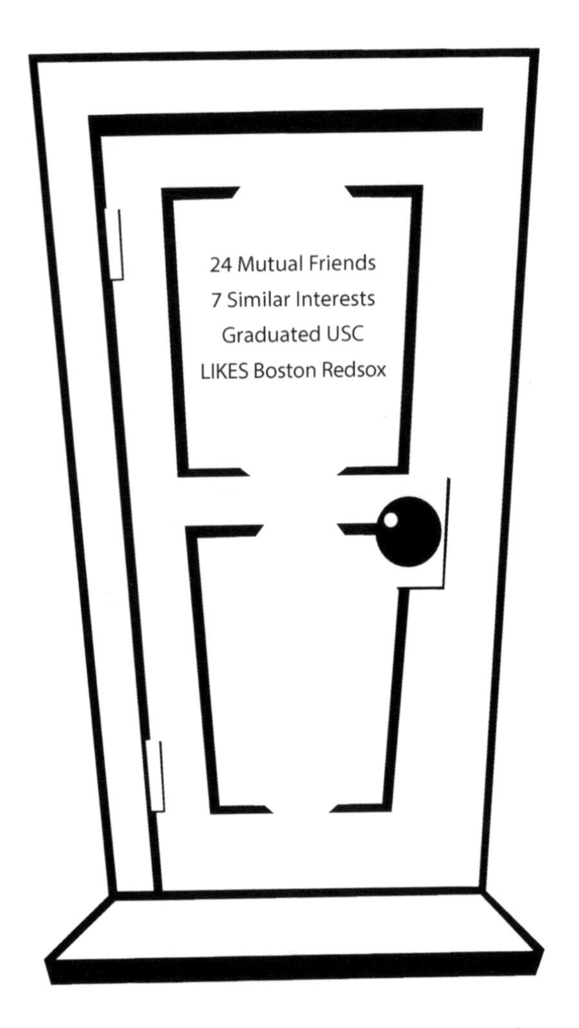

Would you use the information on the front door in your sales pitch when they open the door? Of course you would. Why? Because you just took cold calling and turned it into what? Hot connecting. The door would open, and I would see a lady standing there in the entry way with a name tag on her chest that states

"Sarah Smith," just like we see their "name tag" on Facebook.

> ME: "Hi, Sarah."
> HOMEOWNER: [She sees my same symbolic name tag] "Hi, Tony Giordano, Real Estate Agent here in Beverly Hills, California."

(As I defer to my right and look at the front of her door and start reading it)

> ME: "I'm curious: how do you know these mutual friends of ours, John, Jennifer, Jake, Jill, and Jane? Oh, I see you're a Chicago Bulls fan. How about that game last night?"
> HOMEOWNER: "I know, Tony, I wanted them to win and make the playoffs so bad. I can't believe they lost. I'm from Chicago, so it crushed me."
> ME: "I know, same here. I'm not from Chicago, but just a huge fan. No way, I see you have a dog named Roxy. Oh, is that Roxy? I have a dog named Roxy too. Come here, Roxy. Oh my goodness, she's so adorable. So seriously, how do you know Jill Smith?"
> HOMEOWNER: "Jill is my aunt, actually."
> ME: "Jill is your aunt? Well, I'm sure you of all people, Sarah, know how unbelievable it was to see her go through such a horrible ordeal in her life two years ago and see the way she overcame it and beat it. I have to

tell you, Sarah, your Aunt Jill really inspired me and even made our family stronger."

HOMEOWNER: "Yeah, that's our family. We're fighters, that's for sure. It's kind of a soft subject now, though, because my husband is going through the same illness, and my Aunt Jill has been coming over a lot to help him stay positive and beat it too..."

Do you see how the quality of conversation that would be happening at the front door if the door actually showed you all that information? Why? Because the front door took your six degrees of separation, drew you two together like a magnet, and bonded the two of you way faster than you would have built a bond meeting any other way. **But that doesn't exist in any form of lead generation or prospecting, except online, and very few salespeople are taking advantage of it.** Most are not taking advantage of this extraordinary information that we have at our fingertips today. Only a fraction of top salespeople in America are doing it and doing it well. A fraction? Most salespeople are not seeing the power of how much faster we can build contacts and relationships with real humans online. It's nuts how easy it is. Why? Because you can easily open any conversation with a new human being online—warm, instead of opening "spammy" and cold in any other case. Why on Earth would we ever choose to continue doing anything that's considered cold calling in the world today? Yet I still hear so many speakers, coaches, and trainers presenting on stage at business conferences saying the same things they've been saying for twenty-five years:

> "You've got to get out there and cold call and then follow up with a card and e-mail campaign system with your newsletter..."
> —The Old-Coach-A-Saurus
> (An extinct Dinosaur that was known for its lack of learning new techniques needed to hunt and ultimately died of starvation, along with its following)

"Get out there and cold call"? What? Why? Look at the information that is at our fingertips online today. I know everything about this new contact, simply by adding him as a friend on Facebook or any other similar network. I don't have to cold call this person. I simply have to build a relationship with him and eventually be there for him and whatever needs he has. Oh, and I can do this in a fraction of the time. Literally.

DOOR KNOCKING VERSUS DOOR CLICKING

I can achieve in thirty minutes on Facebook what it would take three hours a day, for fourteen days straight, of door knocking to achieve. I have tracked this stat across the nation with tens of thousands of agents. How many doors do you think you have to knock on today to get five people to give you their e-mail and contact information? The national average is a staggering 265 doors. And 170 of them weren't even home. Would you like to guess how many doors you had to knock on fifteen years ago to get five people to give you their e-mail and contact information? Fewer than thirty. Today it's 265? However, I can go on a social network and, in thirty minutes, engage ten complete strangers in comment threads of posts, send all ten a friend or connection request, log out, and move on with my day. Let's give a low estimate and say only five accept my friend request throughout the day, and now, I don't just have their e-mail, I have their entire life history.

So, does cold calling still work? Sure. However, does it work at the level it once did and have the same ROI it once did? No, it does not.

COLD CALL VERSUS HOT CONNECT

I know what you might be thinking right now. Or at least what I know the doubters out there may be thinking: "Well, Tony, some of the biggest agents and teams in the nation are cold callers. So there."

Yeah, I know most of them too. Want to guess what most of these top agents have? A team (think salaries) of five to ten cold callers (telemarketers) pounding the phones every morning to produce the same results that one agent used to be able to produce fifteen years ago cold calling by him- or herself. Once again, just like door knocking, does it still work? Of course. Every form of lead generation and prospecting works, because you're simply going after what? Numbers, exactly. It doesn't mean it's the most effective form anymore, though, does it? I could send a thousand pigeons in to the sky with my business card tagged to their toes, and I'm sure I'll get a listing out of it. Doesn't mean it's the most effective form of communication anymore, does it? It's funny, but it brings the point home of what I'm talking about.

> "The number-one rule of lead-generation has always been to go where the people are, and where are people today? ONLINE."
> —#TonyG

You see it every day when you walk into the coffee shop. At first you think everyone is praying, but then you realize they are all just on their phones. We know people are not at home to answer the front door as much as they used to be. You knock on the front door of someone under the age of thirty, the person's heart skips a beat. We know many people no longer have land-line phones at their homes to answer telemarketers. You call a cell phone, and no one answers if they don't recognize the phone number. Eventually telemarketers won't be able to hide their company name when they call us. People are online today, period—from the young to the old as well. The number-one demographic creating accounts on multiple networks like Facebook and Twitter are actually senior citizens. Yet, because many businesspeople still have this wall in front of them blocking their ability to have a clear vision and understanding of what online media really can do for their success, many are not taking advantage of it.

LEAD GENERATION VERSUS LEAD ASSUMPTION

Remember in chapter 2 when we discussed lead generation versus lead assumption and knowing the difference? If I am doing *the first thing* (adding people) and *the second thing* (giving them value) every day to have *online presence*, and they start sending me referrals that are closing and increasing my production and income, is that lead generation or lead assumption? Ready for this? It's still lead assumption to me. I have added these people and given them value, *assuming* one day they would send me business. I haven't *lead generated* any of those people yet, but I am still capturing a ton of business. Like I said, *lead assumption* can make you a lot of money too. This only leads me to ask you one thing:

> How much more business could I capture if I purposefully started *lead generating* these people online too?

How easy would it be to send a private message to a random person on Facebook whom you added a couple months ago but is a friend now, because Facebook took that six degrees of separation we discussed and bonded the two of you together? Even if you still have not met him or her in person, you can still open warm in your conversation and eventually lead in to lead generating him or her. Here is another example of the strategies I coach and the power of their effectiveness.

I want you to pretend someone lives at 555 Example Street, Los Angeles, California 00000. Her name is Jane Doe, and she is a successful attorney in your area. One day you are on Facebook doing what I have been telling you to do throughout this book, and a friend of yours posts something, and you see this random lady named Jane Doe, and you engage her and follow it up with a friend request. After three months of liking and commenting on each other's posts and giving each other value, you two feel like you know each other—interests you have, teams she likes that you may hate, where she loves to travel, and so on—and you decide to send her a private message that says something along these lines:

> Hey Jane, how are you? GO 49ers! How do you know Rebecca Smith, anyway? We're going to actually have to meet in person one of these days; this is getting ridiculous. I love seeing pictures of your new puppy—keep them coming.
>
> I'm boosting up my business-to-business marketing database, and I wanted to see how I can add value to what you do for a living and possibly send some of my clients to you. What is your specialty or preferred clientele? Also what is the best way to communicate

> with you, cell or e-mail? Look forward to talking. By the way, if you happen to know anybody looking to buy or sell real estate, we had a goal of helping one hundred families achieve the American dream in 2018 and would love an intro. Have a great day.

What do you think her response would be? How much more likely is this lady going to be open to responding and having further conversation? OK, now for the hammer drop. Forget everything I just said about Facebook and adding Jane Doe as a friend that random day you did. Just pretend it never happened, and you have no idea who she is or anything about her. All I want you to think of is one morning, you're door knocking on Example Street. You walk up to the next house, which is 555 Example Street. You knock, some woman answers the door; it's Jane. But you don't know that, do you? Nope. You don't know anything about her. Good luck with that.

This is only one of many scripts and action plans I've written that have had proven success time and time again. Why do I have many? Because everyone is different. Some have careers, some are retired, some are stay-at-home parents. So the approach needs to be tweaked a little in different scenarios. These techniques are not just for Facebook either. LinkedIn, WhatsApp, WeChat, Instagram, Twitter, Messenger—all are great platforms for lead generation. Why are the preferred ways of communication today texting and social media messaging? You can communicate faster and more effectively. They also have the highest response rate over any other form of communication today. Why do we then make lead generation so much more complicated than it has to be? Using these scripts and communication platforms, on average my coaching clients get a

- ☐ **70 percent+ MRR (message response rate)**
- ☐ **2:40 minutes TTR (time** to **respond rate)**
- ☐ **10 percent+ LRR (lead referral rate)**

This means that for every **one hundred** texts to contacts in their phone, or private messages to digital relationships they've built, or even people they know, they get an average of over **seventy MRR** contacts who respond, who respond in less than **three TTR** minutes, and more than **seven LRR** leads are referred and gained. Oh, and it took a fraction of the time any other form of lead generation would have taken. With a response rate like this, why would we ever continue to **be old** and use **old** forms of communication to reach contacts? Would you ever use **old maps** while driving? That only leads me to ask you this, then:

> "Why are you spending so much time and energy on a form of lead generation or prospecting that is consistently dropping in ROI?"

Act accordingly. Communicate on these modern-day levels. Be accessible on these platforms, because this is what people are doing today. This critical fact—that so many people are on their devices online all day—is what makes the next evolution of lead generation, prospecting, and conversion possible. Would I still door knock? Sure. Would I still call a random number? Sure. I will just choose to use the next evolution of technology in my favor when I do choose to lead generate in those ways. Introducing BIG DATA!

PREDICTIVE ANALYTIC ARTIFICIAL INTELLIGENCE

Just like the algorithms that exist within Facebook, Google, and so many others, there are also companies out there that will help you as a salesperson take advantage of these algorithms in even more effective ways. In other words, how great would it be if there were a company out there that could track all the devices in a territory you would love to capture business from? They would be able to give you a list of homeowners in a territory with nine hundred homes, let's say, and tell you that out of all the homes, here is a list of 187 homeowners in that territory who have been on their household devices clicking on things related to moving or searching for property. Here also are their addresses, phone numbers, social networks, and e-mails.

Well, this is possible today. There are several companies who offer this technology; however, one of these companies has become very popular in the real estate industry because of great innovation and success rates. First, let's have one of the founders of the company, and innovators in the Big Data world, explain predictive analytics a little further.

Big Data, Predictive Analytics, and Real Estate

If you have not heard of Big Data or predictive analytics, then you may want to drop everything and Google it right now. Data will be driving the biggest shifts in how we buy and sell real estate in the next century. Why is data so powerful? Do you remember when you were younger, and you would ask your friend what superpower you would choose if you were a superhero? I am guessing you either chose read people's minds or even predict the future. Well, guess what, you are in luck. Big Data and predictive analytics are predicting the future with extraordinary accuracy. Whether it is predicting the future sales of a home or whether a homeowner is likely to refinance their mortgage—the future is here and it is being predicted.

How does it work? Well, to start it requires a ton of data on past events and behavior. Then it requires a pretty big computer to process billions of variables through a machine-learning algorithm (or what we know as math). The algorithm plays every possible scenario until it finds which one is most likely to happen next. The ability to predict consumer behavior and trends in the market is powerful, but it is not the only piece to the puzzle that will transform real estate. The other piece is how you use the data. Predictive analytics can tell you who is going to buy or sell a home next, but it doesn't take action. In order to turn Big Data into actionable data, you need to implement a strong marketing strategy both online and offline to reach out to homeowners most likely to buy or sell a home.

Of course this is only the beginning. Now that nine out of ten home buyers start online, and all their searches and clicks are being tracked—more data is being collected every second. The Internet is more than just listings on a website—it is a data monster eating every click from every consumer in the entire world. All of this data will be compiled and used to transform how we buy and sell homes, and eventually how we buy and sell everything.

Rich Swier, Cofounder
Offrs LLC
www.offrs.com/sellers (Yes, Offrs without the "e") PROMO CODE: Agent007

Good stuff yet again. I will go a little further and explain this to you in the language of sales rather than language of tech. What Rich was saying here is that when I purchase a territory from them, they will then pull the Big Data from the area and predict who is more than likely getting ready to buy or sell real estate. Mostly sell. An example of this would be as follows.

BIG DATA: "Tony, this property and homeowner are scored at ninety percent likely to sell in the next twelve months."
ME: "How do you know that?"

BIG DATA: "Because homes sell in this neighborhood every 6.7 years on average, and it has been nine years since this property sold."
ME: "Why?"
BIG DATA: "Because homes in this area on average are only 1,650 square feet and are 'starter homes,' and soon, as the family grows in size, they upgrade to a larger home that they will raise their family in for the next twenty-plus years, and we know this property already has two children in elementary school who will soon grow out of this house."
ME: "How do you know they have two children in elementary school?"
BIG DATA: "We match the last names of students in public record transcripts of nearby schools to the last names of public record homeowners in the nearby neighborhood, and we know these students live in this home."
ME: "Oh. Well, what if the house is big enough for them to raise those two kids?"
BIG DATA: "Probably is. But because the mother is pregnant now, it's not likely they will stay there anymore."
ME: "How do you know she's pregnant?"
BIG DATA: "Because the devices that belong to the female in that household have only been clicking on things related to maternity for the last sixty-seven days."
ME: "Where can I buy a territory with you?" Lol.

Predictive analytics and technology like this are here. Is it scary? Sure. Do you think it's scary to me? Yes, it is. Do you think I am going to take full advantage of it to increase my business while I can? Without question, yes! Should you also? *Yes!* But do not even bother with integrating a system like Offrs in your business if you don't have the strong desire to be the *king* or *queen* of your Jungle of Business. Systems like this are not for sheep. They are for lions. Meaning hunters. Meaning lead generators. I often compare lead generation and prospecting to hunting, because you will starve if you do not do it well. Actually, people shouldn't even bother doing most of what I said to do in this book if they are not hunters. Hunters survive. They don't quit, ever. They don't take a break and get lazy because of bad weather. They constantly adapt to their surroundings and find new ways that are more effective to hunt their prey, often finding the path of least resistance.

Whether the market and economy are great for your business or you enter the next "shift," you never stop lead generating. You never quit. If anything, you adapt and hunt smarter. You think a lion chasing its prey slows down and quits because it stepped in a pile of *shift*? ☺ You see, everyone wants to be a lion until it's time to do what real lions do: *hunt*.

> **"You stand above your competition. Not alongside them."**
> —Tony Giordano

resources for your business

Here are resources and systems I personally use in my business and with many of my coaching clients. The biggest and best agents in the world use many of these as well. They use them because they work—and work well. Leverage is not cheap, so if you can find a system that leverages you, it is always worth investing in your business with it. They have also kindly provided discount links and/or codes for you.

WEBSITE CREATION AND LAUNCH: (MULTI-INDUSTRY)
Mopro Inc.
DISCOUNT LINK: www.realestate.mopro.com
PROMO CODE: VIPAgent

LUXURY REAL ESTATE MARKETING AND ADVERTISING AGENCY
The Opulent Agency
WEBSITE LINK: www.theopulentagency.com

LUXURY REAL ESTATE MAGAZINE (LUXURY REAL ESTATE)

duPont Registry Magazine

DISCOUNT LINK: www.dupontregistry.com/xclub

PROMO CODE: Text **797979** the word **XClub** and your **e-mail address**

LISTINGS: PREDICTIVE ANALYTIC LEAD GENERATION (REAL ESTATE)

Offrs (without the "e")

DISCOUNT LINK: www.offrs.com/sellers PROMO CODE: Agent007

"EXPIRED LISTING" CALL LISTS (REAL ESTATE)

LANDVOICE

DISCOUNT LINK: www.landvoice.com/agentvoice

"EXPIRED LISTING" CALL LISTS (REAL ESTATE)

VULCAN 7

DISCOUNT LINK: www.vulcan7.com/ltd17

ONLINE LEAD CAPTURE, POSTING, AND ADVERTISING (MULTI-INDUSTRY)

RALLY APP

DISCOUNT LINK: www.rallyre.com/frenzy18

PROMO CODE: Frenzy18

SOCIAL MEDIA AUTO POSTING (MULTI-INDUSTRY)

City Blast

DISCOUNT LINK: www.cityblast.com/agentblast

PROMO CODE: Agent Blast

CRM AND DATABASE CONVERSION (MULTI-INDUSTRY)

Happy Grasshopper (HG Touch)

DISCOUNT LINK: www.GetHGNow.com

VIRTUAL ASSISTANT (MULTI-INDUSTRY)

My Out Desk (MOD)

DISCOUNT LINK: www.myoutdesk.com/va23

PROFIT AND LOSS / EXPENSE TRACKING (MULTI-INDUSTRY)

ReProphet

DISCOUNT LINK: www.reprophetdiscount.com

DISCOUNT CODE: **ProfitCFO**

Here is a QR to go straight to my resource page on my website, www.giordano.global/resources

about the author

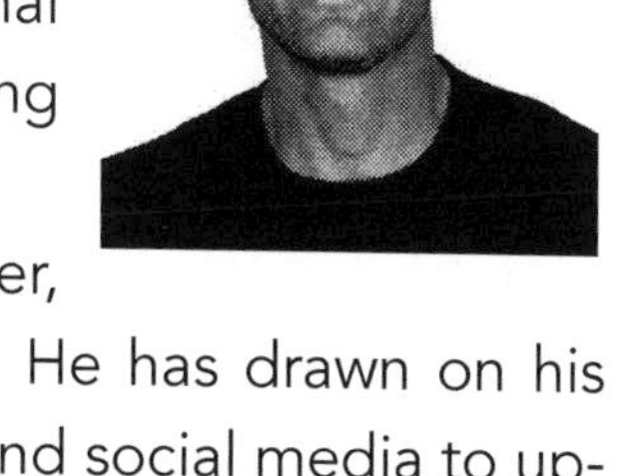

Tony Giordano is a recognized John C. Maxwell 2016 World Top 100 Leader. The first edition of his book *The Social Agent* achieved a national and international best-selling ranking on Amazon.

Giordano is a national speaker, entrepreneur, and business owner. He has drawn on his experience with marketing, sales, and social media to update *The Social Agent* for today's digital media landscape.

Are you still here?

Why are you still here?

Go...

It's over.

The book is over.

Go lead-gen.

Go on now.

Go build your business.

To be continued...